CLINICIAN'S GUIDES

The *Clinician's Guide* series is another American Academy of Oral Medicine educational service. Other titles in this series available from the Academy include:

Treatment of Common Oral Conditions, 6/e

Tobacco Cessation

Oral Health in Geriatric Patients, 2/e

Pharmacology

Chronic Orofacial Pain, 2/e

Oral Cancer

Oral Diseases in Children

CLINICIAN'S GUIDE

Oral Health in Geriatric Patients

Second Edition

Jonathan A. Ship, DMD

Professor, Department of Oral and Maxillofacial Pathology, Radiology, and Medicine
Director, Bluestone Center for Clinical Research
New York University College of Dentistry
Professor, Department of Medicine
New York University School of Medicine
New York, New York

Co-Editors

Jane C. Atkinson, DDS

Chair and Professor, Comprehensive Care and Therapeutics
Executive Director, Clinical Affairs
University of Maryland Dental School
Baltimore, Maryland

Peter L. Jacobsen, PhD, DDS

Professor, Dept of Pathology and Medicine
Director of the Oral Medicine Clinic
University of the Pacific
Arthur A. Dugoni Dental School
San Francisco, California

Abdel R. Mohammad, DDS, MS, MPH

Professor, Department of Geriatrics and Primary Care
Director, Community Outreach and Engagement Programs
Director, Geriatric Dentistry Program
Ohio State University College of Dentistry
Columbus, Ohio

Mahvash Navazesh, DMD

Chair and Associate Professor, Division of Diagnostic Sciences
Director, Office of Medical Affairs
University of Southern California School of Dentistry
Los Angeles, California

Lauren L. Patton, DDS

Professor, Department of Dental Ecology
Director, General Practice Residency Program
School of Dentistry
University of North Carolina at Chapel Hill
Chapel Hill, North Carolina

2006
BC Decker Inc
Hamilton

BC Decker Inc
P.O. Box 620, L.C.D. 1
Hamilton, Ontario L8N 3K7
Tel: 905-522-7017; 800-568-7281
Fax: 905-522-7839; 888-311-4987
E-mail: info@bcdecker.com
www.bcdecker.com

04 05 06 07/WPC/9 8 7 6 5 4 3 2 1

ISBN 1-55009-330-4
Printed in the United States

Sales and Distribution

United States
BC Decker Inc
P.O. Box 785
Lewiston, NY 14092-0785
Tel: 905-522-7017; 800-568-7281
Fax: 905-522-7839; 888-311-4987
E-mail: info@bcdecker.com
www.bcdecker.com

Canada
BC Decker Inc
50 King Street East
P.O. Box 620, LCD 1
Hamilton, Ontario L8N 3K7
Tel: 905-522-7017; 800-568-7281
Fax: 905-522-7839; 888-311-4987
E-mail: info@bcdecker.com
www.bcdecker.com

Foreign Rights
John Scott & Company
International Publishers' Agency
P.O. Box 878
Kimberton, PA 19442
Tel: 610-827-1640
Fax: 610-827-1671
E-mail: jsco@voicenet.com

Japan
Igaku-Shoin Ltd.
Foreign Publications Department
3-24-17 Hongo
Bunkyo-ku, Tokyo, Japan 113-8719
Tel: 3 3817 5680
Fax: 3 3815 6776
E-mail: fd@igaku-shoin.co.jp

UK, Europe, Scandinavia, Middle East
Elsevier Science
Customer Service Department
Foots Cray High Street
Sidcup, Kent
DA14 5HP, UK
Tel: 44 (0) 208 308 5760
Fax: 44 (0) 181 308 5702
E-mail: cservice@harcourt.com

Singapore, Malaysia, Thailand, Philippines, Indonesia, Vietnam, Pacific Rim, Korea
Elsevier Science Asia
583 Orchard Road
#09/01, Forum
Singapore 238884
Tel: 65-737-3593
Fax: 65-753-2145

Australia, New Zealand
Elsevier Science Australia
Customer Service Department
STM Division
Locked Bag 16
St. Peters, New South Wales, 2044
Australia
Tel: 61 02 9517-8999
Fax: 61 02 9517-2249
E-mail: stmp@harcourt.com.au
www.harcourt.com.au

Mexico and Central America
ETM SA de CV
Calle de Tula 59
Colonia Condesa
06140 Mexico DF, Mexico
Tel: 52-5-5553-6657
Fax: 52-5-5211-8468
E-mail: editoresdetextosmex@
prodigy.net.mx

Brazil
Tecmedd Importadora E
Distribuidora De Livros Ltda.
Avenida Maurílio Biagi, 2850
City Ribeirão, Ribeirão Preto –
SP – Brasil
CEP: 14021-000
Tel: 0800 992236
Fax: (16) 3993-9000
E-mail: tecmedd@tecmedd.com.br

India, Bangladesh, Pakistan, Sri Lanka
Elsevier Health Sciences Division
Customer Service Department
17A/1, Main Ring Road
Lajpat Nagar IV
New Delhi – 110024, India
Tel: 91 11 2644 7160-64
Fax: 91 11 2644 7156
E-mail: esindia@vsnl.net

DEDICATION

This volume is dedicated to the memory of Professor Irwin I. Ship. His legacy of teaching, research, patient care, and leadership in the field of oral medicine has been inspirational to generations of practitioners and academicians.

DEDICATION

CONTENTS

AMERICAN ACADEMY OF ORAL MEDICINE

Oral medicine is the specialty of dentistry responsible for the oral health care of medically compromised patients and for the diagnosis and management of medically related disorders or conditions affecting the oral and maxillofacial region.

GOAL: Oral medicine seeks to improve the quality of life of ambulatory and nonambulatory patients with chronic, recurrent, and medically related disorders of the oral and maxillofacial region.

SCOPE: Oral medicine is a nonsurgical specialty that includes the physical evaluation, diagnosis, and therapeutic management of and research into medically related oral diseases such as

1. Salivary gland and functional disorders of the stomatognathic system
2. Chemosensory and neurologic impairment of the oral and maxillofacial complex
3. Orofacial disorders and complications resulting from systemic disease, aging, immunosuppression, and, secondary to drug side effects, radiotherapy, chemotherapy, and hospitalization

AAOM ORAL MEDICINE VISION STATEMENT

The practice of oral medicine enables optimal health to all people through the diagnosis and management of oral diseases. Fundamental to this vision are

- Recognition of the interaction of oral and systemic health
- Integration of medicine and oral health care
- Management of pharmacotherapeutics necessary for treatment of oral and systemic diseases
- Investigation of the etiology and treatment of oral diseases through basic science, oral epidemiology, and clinical research
- Research, teaching, and patient care
- Provision of care for the medically complex patients, the elderly, and those undergoing cancer therapy
- Prevention, diagnosis, and management for the following disorders to include salivary gland diseases, orofacial pain and other neurosensory disorders, and oral mucous membranes

The American Academy of Oral Medicine (AAOM) achieves these goals by holding one or more national meetings annually; by presenting lectures, workshops, and seminars; by promoting research excellence by sponsoring the Lester Burket Student Award and the Robert I. Schattner Abstract Presentations; by sponsoring a section in the *Journal of Oral Surgery, Oral Medicine, Oral Pathology, Oral Radiology and Endodontics*; and by sponsorship of the American Board of Oral Medicine.

PREFACE

The second edition of the American Academy of Oral Medicine *Oral Health in Geriatric Patients* provides an updated and concise summary of the influence of aging, and systemic disease, and its treatment on oral health. This guide is designed for oral health practitioners to be used in their practices as an adjunct in the care of their older patients. It is important for clinicians to reliably recognize, diagnose, and treat oral conditions in the elderly reliably, as well as be aware that aging *and* systemic diseases and their treatments can influence oral health and function. This guide also provides a summary of the etiology, clinical appearance, and treatment of common oral conditions that affect older populations. Topical and systemic drug regimens are provided for the management of common oral disorders. Finally, recommendations are provided on the use of pharmacotherapeutic regimens in the elderly since drug absorption, distribution, metabolism, and excretion are altered in the elderly, and older adults are at risk of adverse drug reactions.

I am indebted to the co-editors of this monograph (Drs. Jane Atkinson, Peter Jacobsen, Abdel Mohammad, Mahvash Narazesh, and Lauren Palton), who have generously shared their expertise in a user-friendly format to advance the practice of geriatric oral health care.

We hope you find this monograph a useful resource in your daily practice.

For the Editors
Jonathan A. Ship, DMD
New York
December 2005

Standard Abbreviations

i	one
ii	two
iii	three
ā	before
ac	before meals (ante cibum)
ad lib	as desired (ad libitum)
asap	as soon as possible
AAOM	American Academy of Oral Medicine
bid	twice a day (bis in die)
btl	bottle
c̄	with
cap	capsule
CBC	complete blood count
CDC	United States Centers for Disease Control and Prevention
crm	cream
disp	dispense on a prescription label
elix	elixir
FDA	United States Food and Drug Administration
g	gram
gtt	drop
h	hour
hs	at bedtime (hora somni)
HSV	herpes simplex virus
IU	international unit
IV	intravenous
L	liter
liq	liquid
loz	lozenge
mg	milligram
min	minute
mL	milliliter
NaF	sodium fluoride
oint	ointment
OTC	over-the-counter
oz	ounce
p	after
pc	after meals (post cibum)

PABA	para-aminobenzoic acid
PHN	postherpetic neuralgia
PLT	platelet count
po	by mouth (per os)
prn	as needed (pro re nata)
q	every
q2h	every 2 hours
q4h	every 4 hours
q6h	every 6 hours
q8h	every 8 hours
q12h	every 12 hours
qam	every morning
qd	every day (quaque die)
qhs	every bedtime
qid	four times a day (quarter in die)
qod	every other day
qpm	every evening
qsad	add a sufficient quantity to equal
qwk	every week
RAS	recurrent aphthous stomatitis
RAU	recurrent aphthous ulcer
RBC	red blood cell count
RHL	recurrent herpes labialis
RIH	recurrent intraoral herpes
Rx	prescription
ś	without
Sig	patient dosing instructions on prescription label
sol	solution
SPF	sun protection factor
stat	immediately
syr	syrup
tab	tablet
tbsp	tablespoon
tid	three times a day (ter in die)
top	topical
tsp	teaspoon
U	unit
ut dict	as directed (ut dictum)
UV	ultraviolet
visc	viscous
VZV	varicella-zoster virus
WBC	white blood cell count
wk	week
yr	year
Zn	zinc

1

ORAL MEDICINE AND GERIATRICS

The geriatric population is the most rapidly growing segment of the population. Aging and systemic diseases and their treatments can influence oral health and function, and it is important for clinicians to be able to recognize, diagnose, and treat oral conditions in the elderly. The purpose of the American Academy of Oral Medicine *Oral Health in Geriatric Patients* is to provide a summary of the influence of aging, systemic disease, and its treatment on oral health. This guide will also provide a summary of the etiology, clinical appearance, and treatment of common oral conditions that affect older populations. Topical and systemic drug regimens are provided for the management of common oral disorders. It is important to remember that the pharmacokinetics of drug absorption, distribution, metabolism, and excretion are altered in the elderly, and therefore the clinician should consider changing drug regimens or dosages depending upon concomitant drug therapy, renal and liver function, and the potential for adverse drug reactions.

THE GERIATRIC POPULATION

The aging population is the most rapidly growing segment of most developed countries. In 1950, only ~10% of the US population was aged 65 years or older. This value increased to 13% in 1997 and is expected to reach 20% by the year 2030. These demographic trends are even more remarkable for very old adults: individuals aged 85+ years will undergo nearly a threefold increase in the next 35 years. In comparison with statistics from 1900, the population has changed dramatically around the world. For example, the median age of death has reached 80 years in the United States (in 1900, the value was 58 years) and 1.5% of the population survives to age 100 (in 1900, the value was 0.03%).

Although most of the world's elderly population live at least partially independent lives, a significant number of older adults are completely dependent for all aspects of life. For example, over 6% of adults in the United States over age 65 years are in nursing homes, currently exceeding 2 million persons. Nursing home residents have more than doubled since 1965, and US nursing home beds exceed hospital beds. The lifetime risk for institutionalization is 52% for females and

30% for males. These trends in the aging population, both community-dwelling independent and institutionalized, have profound implications for oral health, including the status of the natural dentition.

Oral health is particularly important among the elderly. Older adults are more susceptible to systemic conditions, predisposing them to develop oral and maxillofacial diseases that can directly or indirectly lead to malnutrition, altered communication, increased susceptibility to infectious diseases, and diminished quality of life.

Age alone does not seem to play a major role in impaired oral health. Rather, oral diseases (eg dental caries, gingivitis and periodontitis, oral mucosal diseases, salivary dysfunction, alveolar bone resorption), systemic conditions (eg, diabetes, stroke, Alzheimer's disease), prescription and nonprescription medications, and head and neck radiotherapy predispose older persons to developing oral and pharyngeal disorders. The effects of stomatologic diseases are not limited to the oral cavity and its functions. Oral diseases give rise to pathogens, which can be bloodborne or aspirated into the lungs, bringing about severe, even life-threatening consequences. Systemic mucocutaneous and dermatologic diseases can manifest initially in the oral cavity, which can predispose older individuals to additional oral and pharyngeal problems.

Today's older adult is more likely to have natural teeth compared with previous aged cohorts. Thus, older persons are currently at higher risk of developing a serious dentally derived systemic disease than earlier cohorts of elders. In addition, older adults are more likely to utilise dental health care services and perform regular oral hygiene compared with previous older generations. Therefore, the dental profession must be able to diagnose, manage, and ultimately prevent oral diseases that may increase morbidity and mortality among the elderly.

TEETH

The most common age-related changes in teeth include occlusal attrition, pulpal recession and fibrosis, and decreased cellularity. Secondary and reparative dentin contribute progressively to acellular and dehydrated dentin. Hypercementosis is a response to trauma, caries, and periodontal diseases. With greater age, teeth undergo staining, chipping, and cracking and become more susceptible to fracture.

Older people are at risk of developing new and recurrent coronal caries, and they are more likely to have root surface caries compared with younger adults. Dental caries is the most common cause of tooth loss in the elderly, accounting for more extractions than periodontal diseases. Gingival recession, salivary gland hypofunction, less effective oral hygiene, and diminished oral motor function all contribute to root surface caries. Removable prostheses also increase susceptibility to root surface decay. A greater retention of the dentition among the elderly combined with large restorations places coronal surfaces at risk of decay as well.

Caries treatment in the elderly does not differ dramatically from that of younger patients. Fluoride-releasing restorative materials (glass ionomers) are particularly useful for root surface decay and in patients with a dry mouth. Composite resins are indicated for repairing defective restorations and/or carious tooth surfaces, while the new generation of glass ionomer liners provides sustained fluoride release that reduces the incidence of recurrent caries.

An assessment of caries risk is advised for all patients; risk factors found in the geriatric population include use of multiple medications (especially medications that inhibit salivation), gingival recession, and poor oral hygiene secondary to debilitation. Dental caries and subsequent tooth loss can be prevented in high-risk patients with regular recall; application of topical fluoride rinses, gels, and varnishes; appropriate oral hygiene; and early intervention of salivary dysfunction. Older patients with cognitive and/or motor disturbances usually require daily assistance to maintain the health of their dentition.

PERIODONTAL TISSUES

Gingival recession and loss of periodontal attachment and bony support are essentially universal in most older persons. Yet changes in the periodontium attributed solely to age are not sufficient to lead to tooth loss. Nevertheless, because multiple oral factors, systemic diseases, and medications have an adverse influence on periodontal health, and because these conditions are more prevalent among older adults, it is the older population that is at risk of experiencing periodontal disease–related morbidity. For example, patients with diabetes have a higher prevalence and severity of periodontal diseases. Several medications frequently prescribed in older people have been associated with gingival enlargement: antihypertensive calcium channel blockers, the antiseizure drug phenytoin, and the immunosuppressant cyclosporin.

Periodontal diseases have oral and systemic effects on the health of older persons. They have been associated with halitosis, gingivitis, and tooth loss, which can affect mastication, swallowing, tasting, and nutritional intake. Periodontal diseases have also been associated with cardiovascular, cerebrovascular, endocrine, pulmonary, and infective diseases. The treatment of periodontal diseases among the elderly is similar to that for younger patients. Although wound healing may take slightly longer, ultimate disease resolution can be obtained with appropriate interventional therapy and regular oral hygiene. Patients with bleeding disorders, extensive cardiopulmonary problems, and immunosuppression may be poor candidates for periodontal surgery; local methods (extensive scaling/root planing), topical drugs (antimicrobial and anti-inflammatory agents), and occasionally systemic drugs (antimicrobial and anti-inflammatory agents) are preferred.

ORAL MUCOSA

Both normal aging changes and pathologic factors contribute to oral pathoses. Stratified squamous epithelium becomes thinner, loses elasticity, and atrophies with age, while declines in immunologic responsiveness increase susceptibility to infection and trauma. Increases in the incidence of oral and systemic diseases and the use of multiple medications lead to oral mucosal disorders among the elderly. The oral mucosa is a common site for vesiculobullous, desquamative, ulcerative, lichenoid, infectious, and malignant lesions. For example, many older adults are at risk of developing oral fungal infections, which, when diagnosed appropriately, can frequently resolve with topical therapies. Oral cancer is primarily a disease of adults aged 50 years and older, which has only 50% survival at 5 years, owing in part to late diagnosis.

Any mucosal lesion that persists for 3 to 4 weeks despite all attempts to remove suspected etiologies (eg, ill-fitting denture flange) must be thoroughly investigated to determine a diagnosis (eg, biopsy). Regularly scheduled periodic head, neck, and oral examinations are required to diagnose oral mucosal diseases at an early stage and to intervene with appropriate therapy. Importantly, even edentulous older adults require at least an annual head, neck, and oral examination to evaluate for benign and malignant lesions.

SALIVARY GLANDS

Research studies have demonstrated that in healthy older adults, there is no general diminution in the volume of saliva produced. However, many older persons complain of a dry mouth (xerostomia) and have diminished salivary output (salivary hypofunction). Systemic diseases, medications, and radiation therapy for head and neck tumors most likely cause these problems. Over 400 drugs have been reported to decrease salivary flow, especially tricyclic antidepressants, sedatives and tranquilizers, antihistamines, antihypertensives, cytotoxic agents, and anti-Parkinson drugs. Diseases such as Sjögren's syndrome, other autoimmune conditions, diabetes, and Alzheimer's disease can also cause salivary disorders.

Salivary hypofunction leads to numerous oral and pharyngeal problems in the older adult: dry and friable oral mucosa, decreased antimicrobial activity, diminished lubrication, caries development, oral fungal infections, pain, difficulty with mastication, deglutition, gustation, and impaired retention of removable prostheses. Therefore, early diagnosis and intervention are necessary to prevent the deleterious sequelae of a dry mouth. Diagnostic procedures include a careful review of the patient's history and physical findings, sialometry, sialograms, labial gland biopsies, and ^{99m}Tc pertechnetate scintiscans. Consultation with patients' physicians may help change drugs or drug dosages associated with xerostomia. Salivary substitutes; frequent oral hygiene; gustatory, masticatory, and pharmacologic salivary stimulants; and long-term fluoride therapy are required to maintain oral and pharyngeal health for the lifetime of the patient.

ORAL MOTOR AND SENSORY FUNCTION

Alterations in mastication, swallowing, and oral muscular posture occur with aging. The most often reported oral motor disturbance in older people is altered mastication, and even fully dentate older persons are less able to prepare food for swallowing as efficiently as younger adults. This altered masticatory ability may not have any adverse effects on a healthy older person; however, systemic diseases (eg, strokes, Parkinson's disease) and drug regimens (eg, association between tardive dyskinesia and phenothiazines) common in the elderly can cause significant effects on chewing and swallowing, predisposing these persons to choking or aspiration. Other age-related diseases such as osteoarthritis may affect the temporomandibular joint (TMJ), yet the elderly are less likely to report symptoms of TMJ-related pain.

Many older adults complain of diminished food recognition and enjoyment, as well as altered smell and taste function. Research studies have demonstrated that whereas taste function undergoes relatively few age-related changes, smell is dramatically diminished across the human life span. Decreased smell capacity combined with changes in oral motor, salivary, and other sensory modalities most likely accounts for the loss of flavor perception and interest in food in older persons. Medically compromised older adults suffering from these problems require nutritional counseling to prevent malnutrition, dehydration, and a diminished quality of life.

ADDITIONAL READINGS

Abrams WB, Beers MH, Berkow R, editors. The Merck manual of geriatrics. 3rd ed. Rahway: Merck and Co, Inc; 2000.

Barnes IE, Walls A, editors. Gerodontology. Oxford: Wright; 1994.

Hayslip B, Panek P. Adult development and aging. 3rd ed. Malabar: Krieger; 2002.

Hazzard WR, Blass JP, Halter JB, et al, editors. Principles of geriatric medicine and gerontology.5th ed. [In press]

Holm-Pedersen P, Löe H, editors. Textbook of geriatric dentistry. 2nd ed. Copenhagen: Munksgaard; 1996.

TREATMENT PLANNING FOR THE GERIATRIC PATIENT

Subjective Report

- Date, patient name, age, race, gender
- Referring provider
- Chief complaint (CC)
- History of the present illness (HPI)
- Past medical history (PMH)
  - Significant past illness, hospitalization, surgery
  - Current medical problems
- Medications
  - Prescription
  - Nonprescription
  - Herbal and alternative formulations
  - Medication allergies
- Family history (FH)
- Social history (SH)
- Dental history (DH)
  - Regular or symptom-directed dental care
  - Notable or unusual history

Objective Findings

- Vital signs
- Extraoral head and neck examination
  - Facial asymmetries, lymph nodes
  - Temporomandibular joints, muscles of mastication
  - Other
- Intraoral examinatioin
  - Oral mucosal tissues, posterior oral pharynx, salivary glands, tongue, edentulous regions
  - Teeth and periodontal tissues

- Findings from tests
  - Intraoral and extraoral radiographs
  - Imaging studies (eg, magnetic resonance imaging, computed tomography)
  - Study models
  - Pulp tests
  - Blood and urine tests, biopsies, cultures

Assessment

- Differential diagnosis (if multiple, then number them)
- Conclusions drawn from subjective and objective findings

Plan

- Treatment performed
- Proposed treatment plan including medications, diagnostic tests, or other referrals

TREATMENT PLANNING THE GERIATRIC PATIENT WITH "OSCAR"

This is a comprehensive multidimensional assessment tool for planning dental care for the older patient. The five-item mnemonic OSCAR (Table 2-1) serves to guide the dentist in identifying the dental, medical/pharmacologic, functional, ethical, and fiscal factors that need to be evaluated and weighed before treatment.

TABLE 2-1. CRITICAL FACTORS IN THE EVALUATION AND TREATMENT OF THE OLDER DENTAL PATIENT

Issue	Factors of Concern
Oral	Teeth, restorations, prostheses, periodontium, pulpal status, oral mucosa, occlusion, saliva
Systemic	Normative age changes, medical diagnoses, pharmacologic agents, interdisciplinary communication
Capability	Functional ability, self-care, caregivers, oral hygiene, transportation to appointments, mobility within the dental office
Autonomy	Decision-making ability, dependence on alternative or supplemental decision makers
Reality	Prioritization of oral health, financial ability or limitations, significance of anticipated life span

ADDITIONAL READINGS

Berkey DB, Shay K. General dental care for the elderly. Clin Geriatr Med 1992;8:579–97.

Ettinger RL. The unique oral health needs of an aging population. Dent Clin N Am 1997;41:633–49.

Shay K. Identifying the needs of the elderly dental patient. The geriatric dental assessment. Dent Clin N Am 1994;38:499–523.

GUIDE TO TREATMENT OF COMMON ORAL CONDITIONS

PERIODONTAL DISEASES

Periodontal Disease

ETIOLOGY: Gram-positive and -negative bacteria. Exacerbated in the elderly by diminished motor dexterity (arthritis, stroke) and poor oral hygiene.

APPEARANCE: Gingivitis, inflammation of sulcular epithelium, recession, periodontal pocketing (Figures 3-1 to 3-3)

DIFFERENTIAL DIAGNOSIS: Acute necrotizing ulcerative gingivitis (ANUG), pemphigus, pemphigoid, erosive lichen planus

TREATMENT: Prevention requires daily brushing and flossing. Some patients with compromised dexterity may require modified toothbrushes and other oral hygiene devices to facilitate hygiene.

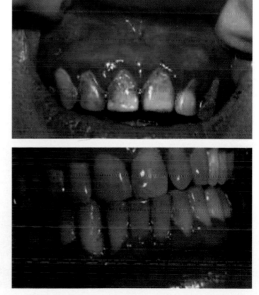

FIGURE 3-1
Marginal gingivitis in a
patient with hypothyroidism.

FIGURE 3-2
Gingivitis and periodontitis.
Vertical bone loss in a patient
with poorly controlled diabetes.

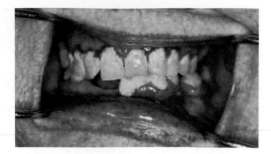

FIGURE 3-3
Periodontal disease and dental neglect in an institutionalized elderly patient with dementia.

Treatment includes the following:

1. Debris removal (scaling, root planing, prophylaxis) and continued personal and intermittent professional hygiene
2. Surgical elimination of periodontal pockets
3. Local antimicrobial therapy (chlorhexidine 0.12% mouthwash or chip, minocycline hydrochloride periodontal microspheres)
4. Systemic antimicrobial drugs (metronidazole 500 mg qid × 10 days, clindamycin 300 mg qid × 10 days, amoxicillin and clavulanate 500 mg tid × 10 days)
5. Systemic anti-inflammatory drugs (doxycycline 20 mg bid)

Patients with immunocompromising and/or bleeding disorders may not be good candidates for surgery. The frequency of oral prophylaxis must be determined on an individual basis and depends on the severity of the periodontal disease and concomitant risk factors. Frequency may range from every month to every 6 months.

Drug-Induced Gingival Enlargement

ETIOLOGY: Calcium channel blockers, phenytoin, cyclosporine

APPEARANCE: Hyperplastic sulcular gingival epithelium with pseudopocketing (Figure 3-4)

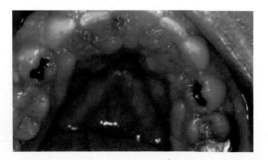

FIGURE 3-4
Gingival enlargement secondary to cyclosporine therapy.

DIFFERENTIAL DIAGNOSIS: Gingivitis, ANUG, leukemic gingival infiltrates

TREATMENT: Improve oral hygiene, surgery (gingivectomy and/or gingivoplasty)

DENTAL CARIES

ETIOLOGY: Gram-positive bacteria (primarily mutans streptococci group and lactobacilli). Risk factors associated with higher rates of caries formation include gingival recession (leading to root caries), salivary hypofunction, use of xerostomic medications, a diet high in fermentable sugars, poor oral hygiene, and inability to perform oral hygiene.

APPEARANCE: Discolored (dark yellow to black) hard to soft lesions on coronal or root surfaces surrounded by decalcified enamel when located on coronal surfaces (Figures 3-5 and 3-6)

DIFFERENTIAL DIAGNOSIS: Calculus; enamel, dentinal, and cemental staining; cervical abrasion or erosion

TREATMENT: When decay is present, it must be removed and replaced with restorative materials. Depending on the location and extent of decay, and especially for root surface caries, fluoride-containing restorative materials should be used. Once the active decay is removed and the teeth restored, treatment should be directed at preventing further decay. For patients with salivary gland hypofunction, see section on salivary gland dysfunction and xerostomia.

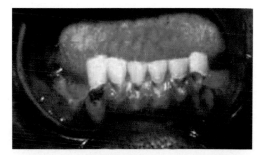

FIGURE 3-5
Severe root surface caries in a patient with Parkinson's disease and drug-induced salivary hypofunction.

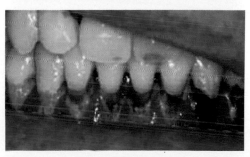

FIGURE 3-6
Root caries in a patient with drug-induced salivary hypofunction.

FLUORIDE PRODUCTS

> **Non-Rx:** 225 ppm NaF rinse, 1,000–1,500 ppm dentifrice

> **Rx:** 5,000 ppm NaF gel and dentifrice, 9,000–12,000 ppm gels/foams (used in dental offices), 22,600 NaF varnish (applied in dental offices)

CARIES PREVENTION FOR ALL PATIENTS
1. Provide oral hygiene instructions.
2. Provide dietary counseling to decrease the frequency of consumption of fermentable carbohydrates.
3. Apply fluoride to teeth (see fluoride products above). Fluoride is available in a variety of formulations and concentrations, and the selection depends on caries risk, the severity of the decay, and the skills or resources available to the patient.
4. Use a non-Rx (over-the-counter [OTC]) fluoride-containing dentifrice after each meal.
5. Use a non-Rx (OTC) fluoride-containing rinse between meals if the patient is unable to brush. Disp: 10 mL. Sig: Rinse and spit 10 mL after meals for 60 seconds and expectorate. Avoid swallowing and rinsing or eating for 30 minutes following rinse.
6. Chew xylitol gum for 5 minutes between meals or after a meal when unable to brush teeth. Use xylitol mints 3 to 4 times daily between meals.

CARIES PREVENTION FOR HIGH-RISK PATIENTS
1. Prescribe a high-concentration fluoride dentifrice. Rx: Neutral pH sodium fluoride gel 1% or neutral pH sodium fluoride gel 1.1% (5,000 ppm). Disp: 1 tube. Sig: Apply a thin ribbon to a toothbrush. Brush thoroughly twice daily for 2 minutes, especially at bedtime. After use, expectorate. For best results, do not eat, drink, or rinse for 30 minutes.
2. Construct a custom fluoride delivery tray. Instruct the patient to place 1 drop of neutral sodium fluoride gel 1.0 or 1.1% per tooth in the custom tray and apply for 5 minutes daily. Avoid rinsing or eating for 30 minutes following treatment.
3. Apply fluoride varnish to teeth every 6 months.
4. Rx: Chlorhexidine 0.12% oral rinse. Disp: 250 mL. Sig: Rinse 15 mL for 30 seconds and expectorate twice daily for 2 weeks.

DENTAL-ALVEOLAR INFECTIONS

ETIOLOGY: Extension of dental caries into pulpal tissues or advanced periodontal disease. Typically caused by pathogens related to dental caries (streptococcal organisms) or periodontal disease.

APPEARANCE: Swelling of the tissues around a tooth, in either a lingual or a buccal direction, sometimes presenting as a fluctuant mass with or without a fistula leading to the source of the infection (Figure 3-7). Pain may be localized to a

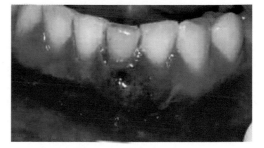

FIGURE 3-7
Dental-alveolar abscess of the
mandibular left lateral incisor.

tooth. May be accompanied by regional adenopathy and fever. Patient should be examined carefully to determine if the infection is localized or has spread beyond the dental-alveolar complex. May spread to the orbit superiorly or into the deep spaces of the neck. Close inspection of the oral tissues is needed to ensure that there is no elevation of the tongue or asymmetry of the posterior pharyngeal structures.

TREATMENT: Endodontic treatment or extraction of the infected tooth; incision or drainage if swelling is fluctuant. Refer to oral surgeon if extensive regional spread is evident. Antibiotic therapy may be necessary. In most cases, antibiotics are prescribed without culture of the area.

> Rx: Penicillin VK, 500 mg.
> Disp: 40 tabs.
> Sig: Take 1 tab q6h for 10 days

> Rx: Clindamycin, 150 mg.
> Disp: 29 tabs.
> Sig: Take 2 tabs stat and then 1 tab qid, for 7 days. The capsule form of clindamycin should be taken with a full glass (8 ounces) of water or with meals to prevent irritation of the esophagus. Contact the doctor if diarrhea develops.

ULCERATIVE LESIONS OF THE ORAL MUCOSA

Traumatic Ulcerations

ETIOLOGY: Lip and cheek biting, factitial, motor dysfunction, pressure necrosis phenomenon, improper toothbrushing, broken teeth, irritation by faulty restorations, or improperly fitting removable prostheses

APPEARANCE: Ulcer with necrotic center, inflamed periphery

DIFFERENTIAL DIAGNOSIS: Aphthous ulcer, primary or secondary syphilis, erosive lichen planus, squamous cell carcinoma, herpes simplex

TREATMENT: Etiology must be identified and removed. If there is no resolution within 3 to 4 weeks (in the elderly, healing may take longer), the lesion must be biopsied. Larger lesions may require topical anesthetics (see the following section).

Oral Mucositis

ETIOLOGY: Oral mucositis or stomatitis describes inflammation of oral mucosa resulting from cytotoxic chemotherapeutic agents or ionizing radiation used primarily to treat malignancy.

Radiotherapy for head and neck tumors may result in radiation dermatitis, mucositis, stomatitis, and oral ulceration. The severity of ulceration depends on the radiation dose and fractionation, the portal of the beam, and the extent of metallic restorations. Initial mucositis occurs during the second week of radiotherapy, and oral mucositis remains a continuing problem despite the variety of agents proposed as treatments. Mucositis is exacerbated by salivary dysfunction, oral candidosis, and malnutrition.

High-dose chemotherapy, such as that used in the treatment of leukemia and hematopoietic stem cell transplant regimens, may produce severe erythematous mucositis. Chemotherapy to treat breast cancer and other solid organ tumors may also result in varying degrees of mucositis. Mucosal breakdown is drug and dose dependent and typically occurs 7 to 10 days following initiation of therapy. Mucositis is self-limited when uncomplicated by infection and typically heals within 2 to 4 weeks after cessation of cytotoxic chemotherapy.

APPEARANCE: Diffuse erythema on all mucosal surfaces, followed by epithelial desquamation and ulceration (Figure 3-8).

DIFFERENTIAL DIAGNOSIS: Oral candidosis, recurrent herpetic stomatitis, erythema multiforme

TREATMENT: Management of salivary dysfunction (see "Salivary Gland Dysfunction and Xerostomia [Dry Mouth]"), management of candidosis (see "Candidosis"); increase fluids and nutrients (eg, Ensure, Sustacal).

Amifostine (200 mg/m² IV or 500 mg SC 30–60 minutes before each dose of radiotherapy) may be effective in reducing radiation mucositis (as well as xeros-

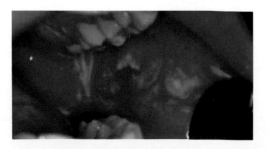

FIGURE 3-8
Severe oral mucositis during the fourth week of external beam radiotherapy for the treatment of a mucoepidermoid carcinoma of the parotid gland.

tomia). Benzydamine oral rinses may also provide relief from mucositis. Keratinocyte growth factor (KGF) and sucking on ice chips may also reduce mucositis in patients receiving chemotherapy.

Patients should be instructed to rinse frequently and continue oral hygiene during radiation therapy with an extra soft toothbrush, which can be softened in warm water if needed. Avoid alcohol-containing mouthwash. Topical analgesics (see below) may provide temporary relief, but many patients will need systemic pain medication.

> Rx: Add ¼ teaspoon baking soda and ⅛ teaspoon salt to 1 cup water.
> Disp: 1 cup.
> Sig: Rinse several times a day, especially after meals.

> Rx: 2% viscous lidocaine HCl.
> Disp: 250 mL.
> Sig: Swish and spit 5 mL for 5 minutes qid for pain.

> Rx: Diphenhydramine 12.5 mg/5 mL elixir.
> Disp: 250 mL.
> Sig: Swish and spit 5 mL qid for 5 minutes.

> Rx: Lidocaine or diphenhydramine can be mixed 1:1 with either kaolin and pectin (Kaopectate), aluminum hydroxide and magnesium hydroxide (Maalox), or sucralfate to increase mucosal binding. If an oral fungal infection is suspected, add nystatin 100,000 U/mL.

Chemical Ulceration

ETIOLOGY: Prescription (eg, chemotherapeutic agents, immunosuppressants) and nonprescription (aspirin burn) medications, nonprecious metals in prosthodontic appliances (cobalt chromium and nickel chromium alloys), acrylic monomer, etching solutions for bonded restorations

APPEARANCE: Localized inflammation, ulcer, or leukoplakic patch that leaves an erythematous and painful area when removed (Figures 3-9 and 3-10)

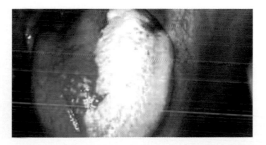

FIGURE 3-9
Chemotherapy-induced ulceration of the tongue and mucosal tissues due to 5-fluorouracil.

FIGURE 3-10
Mucositis after completion of
extrernal beam radiotherapy
and 3 courses of cisplatin
(100 mg) for a laryngeal
squamous cell carcinoma.

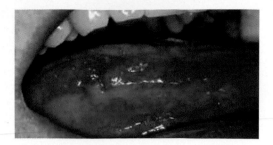

DIFFERENTIAL DIAGNOSIS: Aphthous ulcer, pseudomembranous candidosis, primary or secondary syphilis chancre, squamous cell carcinoma, herpes simplex

TREATMENT: Etiology must be identified and removed. If there is no resolution within 3 to 4 weeks (in the elderly, healing may take longer), the lesion must be biopsied. Larger lesions may require topical anesthetics (see "Oral Mucositis"), topical antimicrobials (see "Oral Mucositis"), and topical corticosteroids (see the following section).

Erosive Lichen Planus

ETIOLOGY: Idiopathic, autoimmune, drug- or virally induced lesion that involves T-cell infiltration of the oral mucosal tissues. May develop secondary to hepatitis C infection. Associated with malignant transformation in a low percentage of cases and may be more frequent with the erosive forms of lichen planus. Diagnosis requires biopsy and may involve other diagnostic testing, such as serologic testing for hepatitis C.

APPEARANCE: May have a variety of appearances. Classically, eroded and ulcerated lesions on all mucosal surfaces (Figure 3-11) with areas of radiating white striae (when lesions consist only of leukoplakic radiating striae, it is referred to as reticular lichen planus; Figures 3-12 and 3-13). Also associated with skin and genital lesions.

DIFFERENTIAL DIAGNOSIS: Recurrent aphthous ulcer, recurrent herpes simplex, pemphigus, pemphigoid, lupus erythematosus, erythema multiforme, candidiasis, squamous cell carcinoma

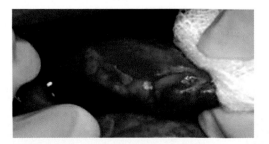

FIGURE 3-11
Erosive lichen planus of the
lateral and dorsal surfaces of
the tongue.

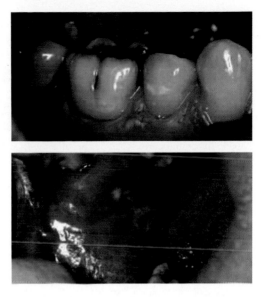

Figure 3-12
Reticular lichen planus of the attached gingival tissues.

Figure 3-13
Reticular lichen planus with Wickham's striae of the buccal mucosa.

TREATMENT: Patients should be advised that the condition is often chronic and may recur when therapy is stopped. The therapeutic objective is to control the disease by reducing inflammation, especially when painful. Oral candidosis may develop in patients chronically using topical steroids. An oral cyclosporine rinse has been reported as a treatment but is extremely costly.

TOPICAL STEROIDS AND IMMUNOSUPPRESSANTS

Rx: Dexamethasone elixir 0.5 mg/5 mL.
Disp: 250 mL.
Sig: Swish and spit 5 mL qid for 5 minutes.

Rx: Clobetasol propionate 0.05% gel.
Disp: 15 g tube.
Sig: Apply to affected regions tid.

Rx: Fluocinonide 0.05% gel.
Disp: 15 g tube.
Sig: Apply to affected regions tid.

Rx: Tacrolimus 0.1% ointment.
Disp: 15 g tube.
Sig: Apply to affected regions tid.

> **Rx:** Betamethasone sodium phosphate-betamethasone acetate 3 mg–3 mg/mL (Celestone Soluspan)
> **Disp:** 0.2 mL intralesional injection.

> **Rx:** Dexamethasone sodium phosphate 4 mg/mL.
> **Disp:** 0.5 mg intralesional injection

NOTE: Injectable steroids can be combined with short-lasting (eg, lidocaine 2%) or longer-lasting (eg, bupivacaine hydrochloride 0.5%) injectable anesthetics to provide pain relief.

SYSTEMIC STEROIDS AND IMMUNOSUPPRESSANTS FOR SEVERE CASES

> **Rx:** Prednisone 5 mg tabs.
> **Disp:** 86 tabs .
> **Sig:** Take 12 tabs qd × 2 days, 10 tabs qd × 2 days, 8 tabs qd × 2 days, 6 tabs qd × 2 days, 4 tabs qd × 2 days, 2 tabs qd × 2 days, 1 tab qd × 2 days. Consider therapy every other day to decrease immunosuppression.

> **Rx:** Azathioprine 50 mg.
> **Disp:** 50 tabs.
> **Sig:** take 1 tab qd × 1 week and then 2 tabs qd × 1 week and then reevaluate (should be used concomitantly with prednisone).

NOTE: For the older patient with diabetes, osteoporosis, uncontrolled cardiovascular diseases, narrow-angle glaucoma, depression, or any other immunocompromising condition, consult with the patient's physician before initiating prednisone therapy. Side effects have occurred more commonly in long-term follow-up of patients taking systemic steroids versus topical steroids, whereas the percentage of patients responding to long-term therapy was the same. Baseline CBC with platelets and liver enzymes are required before initiating azathioprine.

Recurrent Aphthous Ulcer

ETIOLOGY: Local altered immune response. Systemic etiologies include nutritional deficiencies (iron, vitamins B_6 and B_{12}), diabetes mellitus, inflammatory bowel disease, Behçet's disease, Crohn's disease, and immunosuppression. Biopsy will rule out other vesiculoulcerative diseases.

APPEARANCE: Minor aphthous ulcer: < 0.6 cm shallow ulceration with gray pseudomembrane and erythematous halo on nonkeratinized mucosa (Figure 3-14). Major aphthous ulcer: > 0.5 cm ulcer, more painful, lasting several weeks to months; will scar (Figure 3-15)

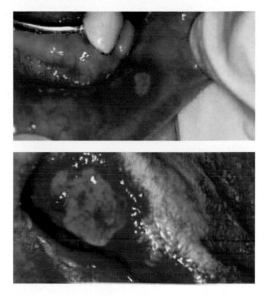

FIGURE 3-14
Minor recurrent aphthous stomatitis in a healthy 51-year-old female.

FIGURE 3-15
Major recurrent aphthous stomatitis nonresponsive to topical and systemic corticosteroids.

DIFFERENTIAL DIAGNOSIS: Herpes simplex virus, chemical or traumatic ulcer, vesiculoulcerative diseases, squamous cell carcinoma, erosive lichen planus, cytomegalovirus infection

TREATMENT: Topical analgesics (see "Oral Mucositis") and topical steroids or immunosuppressants (see "Erosive Lichen Planus"). Localized injections can be helpful for large and painful lesions (see "Erosive Lichen Planus"). Systemic and topical thalidomide has been studied as a treatment in human immunodeficiency virus (HIV)-infected patients with oral aphthous ulcers.

INFLAMMATORY CONDITIONS OF THE ORAL MUCOSA

Inflammatory Papillary Hyperplasia (Papillomatosis)

ETIOLOGY: Poorly fitting denture

APPEARANCE: Multiple small polypoid or papillary lesions, typically on hard palate, that produce a cobblestone appearance

DIFFERENTIAL DIAGNOSIS: Condyloma acuminatum, papilloma, verrucous carcinoma, Cowden disease (intestinal neoplasia, carcinoma or fibrotic disease of the breast, papillary lesions of the skin)

TREATMENT: Discontinue using denture; surgical removal of hyperplastic tissue with scalpel, cautery, or laser. Occasionally, tissue conditioner may reduce the problem, although construction of a new denture may be necessary.

Epulis Fissurata (Inflammatory Fibrous Dysplasia, Denture Granuloma)

ETIOLOGY: Overextended denture flanges or resorption of alveolar bone that make the denture borders overextended

APPEARANCE: Hyperplastic granulation tissue surrounds the denture flange. Pain, bleeding, and ulceration can develop (Figures 3-16 and 3-17).

DIFFERENTIAL DIAGNOSIS: Verrucous carcinoma, squamous cell carcinoma, traumatic fibroma

TREATMENT: Small lesions may resolve if denture flanges are reduced. Surgical excision is necessary prior to rebasing or relining of the denture.

Angular Cheilitis

ETIOLOGY: Diminished occlusal vertical dimension, candidosis, vitamin B or iron deficiency.

APPEARANCE: Wrinkled and sagging skin at the lip commissures with desiccation and mucosal cracking (Figure 3-18)

DIFFERENTIAL DIAGNOSIS: Dry chapped lips, labial herpes simplex virus, basal cell carcinoma, squamous cell carcinoma

TREATMENT:

> Rx: Nystatin/triamcinolone acetonide ointment.
> Disp: 15 g tube.
> Sig: Apply to affected area after each meal and qhs. Concomitant intraoral antifungal treatment may be indicated (see the following section).

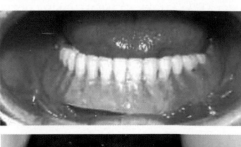

FIGURE 3-16
Denture granuloma (epulis fissuratum).

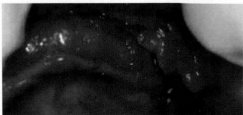

FIGURE 3-17
Denture granuloma (epulis fissuratum).

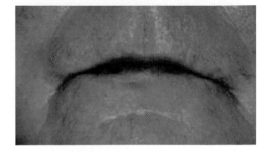

FIGURE 3-18
Angular cheilitis in a patient with a poorly fitting removable prosthesis and salivary hypofunction.

Candidosis

ETIOLOGY: The most common fungal organism isolated from the oral cavity is *Candida albicans*. Risk factors include salivary gland hypofunction; systemic treatment with antibiotics, corticosteroids, immunosuppressants, and cytotoxic agents; and diabetes mellitus and other immunocompromising conditions. Diagnosis requires positive culture, positive smear, or biopsy.

TREATMENT:

> **Rx:** Nystatin oral suspension 100,000 U/mL.
> Disp: 60 mL.
> Sig: Swish and swallow 5 mL qid for 5 minutes. Retain suspension in the mouth as long as possible. Contains sugar.

> **Rx:** Nystatin 100,000 U/g cream or ointment.
> Disp: 15 g tube.
> Sig: Apply thin coat to affected areas after each meal and qhs.

> **Rx:** Nystatin troche 200,000 U.
> Disp: 70 pastilles.
> Sig: Let 1 pastille dissolve in mouth 5 times/day. Do not chew or swallow whole.

> **Rx:** Nystatin 100,000 U vaginal tablet.
> Disp: 70 tabs.
> Sig: Let 1 tab dissolve in mouth 5 times/day. Do not chew or swallow whole. Suitable for the patient with salivary hypofunction because the vaginal suppository does not contain sugar.

> **Rx:** Ketoconazole 2% cream.
> Disp: 15 g tube.
> Sig: Apply thin coat to affected areas after each meal and qhs.

Rx: Clotrimazole 1% cream.
Disp: 15 g tube.
Sig: Apply thin coat to affected areas after each meal and qhs.

Rx: Clotrimazole troches 10 mg.
Disp: 70 troches.
Sig: Let 1 troche dissolve in mouth 5 times/day. Do not chew or swallow whole. Contains sugar.

Rx: Clotrimazole 100 mg vaginal suppository.
Disp: 70 suppositories.
Sig: Let 1 suppository dissolve in mouth 5 times/day. Do not chew or swallow whole. Suitable for the patient with salivary hypofunction because the vaginal suppository does not contain sugar.

Rx for Dentures: Improve oral hygiene of the appliance, keep the denture out of the mouth for extended periods and while sleeping, soak for 30 minutes in solutions containing benzoic acid, 0.12% chlorhexidine, or 1% sodium hypochlorite, and thoroughly rinse. Apply a few drops of nystatin oral suspension or a thin film of nystatin ointment to the inner surface of the denture after each meal.

Rx for Refractory Candidosis: Ketoconazole 200 mg.
Disp: 20 tabs.
Sig: Take 1 tab daily for 10–14 days.

Rx: Fluconazole 100 mg.
Disp: 20 tabs.
Sig: Take 2 tabs stat and then 1 tab daily for 10–14 days.

Rx: Itraconazole 100 mg.
Disp: 20 tabs.
Sig: Take 1 tab bid for 10–14 days. Take capsules with food.

NOTE: In the patient with salivary hypofunction at risk of dental caries, avoid the sugar content of nystatin and clotrimazole troches by substituting with vaginal nystatin tablets or clotrimazole suppositories.

Acute Pseudomembraneous Candidosis (Thrush)

ETIOLOGY: Oral candidosis

APPEARANCE: White slightly elevated plaques that can be wiped away leaving an erythematous base. Direct smear can be fixed and stained using periodic acid–Schiff reagent to reveal the *Candida* hyphae microscopically. In severely debilitated patients, extension of candidosis into the esophagus and trachea may prove fatal (Figures 3-19 to 3-21).

DIFFERENTIAL DIAGNOSIS: Radiation- or chemotherapy-induced mucositis

Acute Atrophic Candidosis (Antibiotic Sore Tongue)

ETIOLOGY: Oral candidosis secondary to antibiotics or steroids

APPEARANCE: Similar to thrush without overlying pseudomembrane erythematous and painful mucosa (Figures 3-22 and 3-23)

DIFFERENTIAL DIAGNOSIS: Erosive lichen planus, chemical erosion

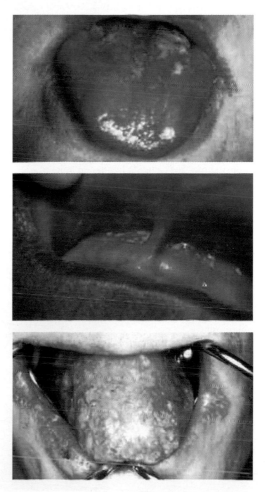

FIGURE 3-19
Atrophic and pseudomembraneous candidosis and angular cheilitis in a patient with poorly controlled diabetes.

FIGURE 3-20
Pseudomembraneous candidosis in an immunosuppressed patient on long-term corticosteroids for systemic lupus erythematosus.

FIGURE 3-21
Acute pseudomembraneous candidosis secondary to antibiotic therapy.

FIGURE 3-22
Atrophic candidosis in a
patient with poorly controlled
diabetes.

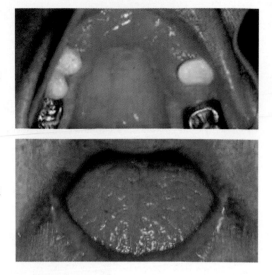

FIGURE 3-23
Acute atrophic candidosis and
angular cheilitis secondary to
antibiotic therapy.

Chronic Atrophic Candidosis (Denture Sore Mouth)

ETIOLOGY: Most common form of oral candidosis; candidal infection of the denture as well. Treatment should be directed toward the mucosa and denture.

APPEARANCE: Mucosa beneath the denture is erythematous with a well-demarcated border. Swabs from the mucosal surface may provide a prolific growth, but biopsy shows few *Candida* hyphae in spite of high serum and saliva antibodies to *Candida* (Figures 3-24 and 3-25).

DIFFERENTIAL DIAGNOSIS: Inflammatory papillary hyperplasia

FIGURE 3-24
Chronic atrophic candidosis
in a patient wearing a metal-
based partial maxillary removable prosthesis.

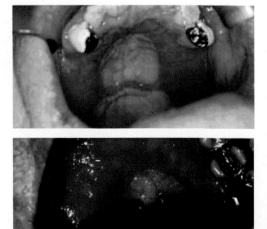

FIGURE 3-25
Chronic atrophic candidosis
(denture stomatitis) in a
patient wearing a partial
metal-based removable
prosthesis.

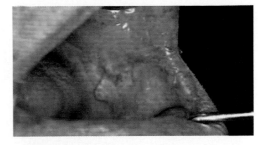

FIGURE 3-26
Chronic hyperplastic candidosis.

Chronic Hyperplastic Candidosis (Candida Leukoplakia)

ETIOLOGY: Oral candidosis; lesion should be considered potentially premalignant. Treatment should be directed toward mucosa and leukoplakia.

APPEARANCE: Confluent leukoplakic plaques characterized by *Candida* invasion of oral epithelium with marked atypia (Figure 3-26).

DIFFERENTIAL DIAGNOSIS: Leukoplakia, dysplasia, carcinoma in situ, squamous cell carcinoma, lichen planus

BURNING MOUTH SYNDROME (GLOSSOPYROSIS, STOMATOPYROSIS)

ETIOLOGY: The most common etiology is idiopathic. It may represent a chronic neuropathic condition, possibly induced by traumatic injury. Ill-fitting dentures may contribute to burning sensations. Other potential etiologies include nutritional deficiencies (vitamins B_1, B_2, B_6, and B_{12} and folic acid), local trauma, gastrointestinal disorders, diabetes, and allergies.

APPEARANCE: The presence of an oral lesion precludes the diagnosis of burning mouth syndrome. Oral candidosis and/or salivary gland dysfunction may be concomitant with findings.

DIFFERENTIAL DIAGNOSIS: After all possible etiologic agents have been eliminated, the diagnosis is established.

TREATMENT: Physical evaluation and laboratory studies should rule out any organic etiology. Minimal blood studies should include CBC and differential, fasting blood glucose, iron, ferritin, folic acid, and vitamin B_{12}.

FOR SYMPTOMATIC RELIEF Topical anesthetic rinses (see "Oral Mucositis").

Rx: Zostrix 0.025% cream.
Disp: 15 g tube.
Sig: Apply minor amounts to local area of burning, tid. Warn patient of a temporary local burn.

Rx: Nortriptyline 10 mg.
Disp: 50 tabs.
Sig: Take 1 tab qhs for 1 week and 2 tabs qhs for 1 week and increase to 3 tabs qhs and maintain dosage.

Rx: Desipramine hydrochloride 25 mg.
Disp: 50 tabs.
Sig: Take 1 tab qhs for 1 week and then 2 tabs qhs for 1 week. Increase to 3 tabs qhs and maintain dosage.

Rx: Clonazepam 0.50 mg.
Disp: 50 tabs.
Sig: Take 1 tab qd for 1 week and then 1 tab bid for 1 week. If necessary, increase to 1 tab tid and maintain dosage.

Rx: Gabapentin 300 mg.
Disp: 90 tabs.
Sig: Take 1 tab on day 1, 1 tab bid on day 2, and 1 tab tid on day 3. Increase further prn symptoms. Max: 3 tabs tid or 2,700 mg. Gabapentin is a useful adjuvant with a tricyclic antidepressant or benzodiazepine.

NOTE: Dosages should be adjusted according to the individual response of the patient. Anticipated side effects include dry mouth and morning drowsiness. The rationale for the use of tricyclic antidepressant medications, benzodiazepines, antiseizure drugs, and other psychotropic drugs should be thoroughly explained to the patient, and the physician should be made aware of this therapy. These medications have a potential for addiction and dependency. Older persons taking concomitant central nervous system depressants should not be prescribed these medications before consulting with the patient's physician.

SALIVARY GLAND DYSFUNCTION AND XEROSTOMIA (DRY MOUTH)

ETIOLOGY: Multiple medications (anticholinergics, antihypertensives, antihistamines, psychotropics, antidepressants, antiparkinsonism agents), head and neck radiation therapy, Sjögren's syndrome (Figures 3-27 and 3-28), autonomic nerve dysfunction

Appearance

Oral mucosa appears dry, pale, or atrophic (Figures 3-29 to 3-31). The tongue may be devoid of papillae with a fissured and inflamed appearance (Figures 3-32 and 3-33). Salivary gland obstructions owing to medication- and disease-induced hypofunction lead to unilateral or bilateral glandular enlargement, fre-

FIGURE 3-27
Bilateral enlarged parotid
glands in a patient with
Sjögren's syndrome.

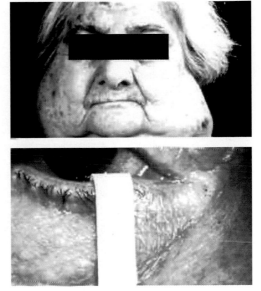

FIGURE 3-28
Schirmer's test to determine
tear production in a patient
with xerophthalmia secondary
to Sjögren's syndrome.

quently during mealtime (Figure 3-34). New and recurrent dental caries and difficulty with chewing, swallowing, and tasting may occur. Fungal infections are common.

TREATMENT:

FOR DRUG-INDUCED DYSFUNCTION Consult with the physician to decrease drug dose, alter drug dosages, or substitute one xerostomic medication for a similar-acting drug with fewer salivary side effects.

SALIVARY SUBSTITUTES Sodium carboxymethyl cellulose 0.5% aqueous solution (OTC). Dispense 8 fl oz. Use as a rinse as frequently as needed. Commercial salivary substitutes (OTC) include Sage Moist-Plus spray, XeroLube, Salivart, MoiStir, Orex, or Optimoist. Commercial oral moisturizing gels (OTC) include Sage Moist-Plus Mouth Moisturizer and Oral Balance.

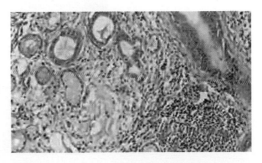

FIGURE 3-29
Histopathology of sialadenitis
in a patient with drug-induced
salivary hypofunction.

Figure 3-30
Severe salivary hypofunction and xerostomia in an edentulous patient taking multiple drugs for hypertension and depression.

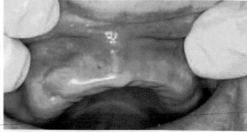

Figure 3-31
Salivary hypofunction and xerostomia in a patient who completed a 7-week course of external beam radiotherapy for a squamous cell carcinoma of the tongue.

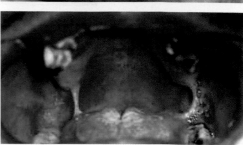

Figure 3-32
Fissured and desicated tongue due to severe salivary hypofunction.

Figure 3-33
Fissured and desicated tongue secondary to radiotherapy-induced salivary hypofunction.

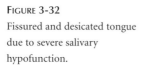
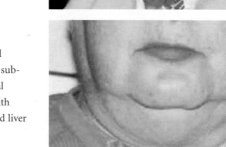

Figure 3-34
Bilateral salivary gland enlargement (parotid, submandibular, sublingual glands) in a patient with chronic alcoholism and liver failure.

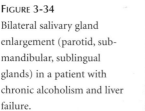

SYMPTOMATIC TREATMENTS Sip water frequently all day long, let ice melt in the mouth, restrict caffeine intake, avoid mouth rinses containing alcohol, humidify the sleeping area, and coat the lips with lubricant.

SALIVARY STIMULANTS Sugarless candies, sugarless mints, and sugarless gums can stimulate saliva from the remaining salivary tissue and may be the most appropriate method of controlling medication-induced salivary hypofunction. Two pharmaceutical agents (cholinergic agonists) can stimulate the remaining functional salivary tissue but will have limited success in patients who cannot produce saliva (such as after significant head and neck radiation for cancer). Patients can take these medications less frequently every day because they are primarily for patient comfort.

> Rx: Pilocarpine HCl 5 mg.
> Disp: 90 tabs.
> Sig: Take 1 tab tid before meals and 1 tab qhs. May need 2–3 months to determine effectiveness. Side effects include sweating, chills, diarrhea, and increased need to urinate. May cause decreased vision in low light. Avoid in patients with narrow-angle glaucoma, severe asthma, and pulmonary diseases. Use carefully in patients taking antihypertensive medications. Also may interfere with the therapeutic actions of many drugs.

> Rx: Cevimeline HCl 30 mg.
> Disp: 60 tabs.
> Sig: Take 1 tablet tid. Dose may be raised to 45 mg tid. Discontinue if no positive effect in 3 months. Side effects and precautions are the same as those for pilocarpine. This cholinergic agonist has a longer half-life; therefore, only three doses/day are needed.

NOTE: Patients are at risk of developing caries (see "Dental Caries") and oral fungal infections (see "Candidosis"). Consult with the patient's physician prior to prescribing these drugs if the patient is taking multiple medications.

VESICULOBULLOUS LESIONS OF THE ORAL MUCOSA

Pemphigus Vulgaris and Cicatricial Pemphigoid

ETIOLOGY: Autoimmune diseases with autoantibodies appearing in different portions of the epidermis/mucosa. In pemphigus, the autoantibodies are within the epithelium in the prickle cell layer. In pemphigoid, autoantibodies are located at the basement membrane. Diagnosis is based on the history, clinical presentation, histopathology, direct and indirect immunofluorescent studies of biopsy specimens, and, in some cases, autoantibody studies using serum

APPEARANCE:

PEMPHIGUS Small flaccid bullae can occur on any oral mucosal site and will rupture, leaving an ulcer (Figure 3-35). Nikolsky's sign is positive but not confirmatory for diagnosis. Approximately 80 to 90% of patients have oral lesions, and oral manifestation may be the first sign of systemic disease.

PEMPHIGOID Oral bullae on any mucosal site that may be intact longer than in pemphigus. Bullae subsequently rupture and leave a large ulcer (Figure 3-36). Lesions can scar, and ocular lesions may coexist with oral lesions, necessitating referral to an ophthalmologist. Approximately one-third of pemphigoid patients have oral lesions.

DIFFERENTIAL DIAGNOSIS: Lichen planus, major aphthous ulcer, lupus erythematosus, erythema multiforme

TREATMENT: Topical anesthetics (see "Oral Mucositis") and topical steroids (see "Erosive Lichen Planus").

For patients with lesions limited to the palatal mucosa and gingiva, custom mouthguards can be constructed for applying topical steroids 15 to 30 minutes tid. For localized nonhealing lesions, injectable steroids can be useful (see "Erosive Lichen Planus"). Use systemic steroids and immunosuppressants for severe cases (see "Erosive Lichen Planus").

Two other drugs have been added to steroid and immunosuppressant protocols with moderate success: mycophenolate mofetil for pemphigus and dapsone for pemphigoid.

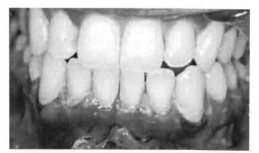

FIGURE 3-35
Pemphigus vulgaris ulcerative lesions in a 63-year-old female.

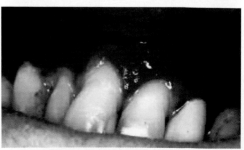

FIGURE 3-36
Cicatricial pemphigoid erosive lesions affecting the interdental papillae and attached gingival tissues.

Varicella Zoster (Herpes Zoster, Shingles)

ETIOLOGY: Reactivation of latent herpes varicella-zoster virus present since an original infection (chickenpox). Precipitating factors include thermal, inflammatory, radiologic, or mechanical trauma and immunocompromising states, including cancer, lymphoma, and Hodgkin's disease. Occurs more commonly in the elderly.

APPEARANCE: Painful segmental eruption of small vesicles that rupture to form confluent ulcers. Vesicles appear on the skin and oral mucous membranes and occur unilaterally along the ophthalmic, maxillary, or mandibular divisions of the trigeminal nerve (Figure 3-37). Ophthalmic division involvement requires close monitoring by an ophthalmologist. Postherpetic neuralgia can last for months following eruption of vesicles.

DIFFERENTIAL DIAGNOSIS: Herpes simplex, erythema multiforme

TREATMENT:

> Rx: Valacyclovir HCl 500 mg.
> Disp: 60 tab.
> Sig: Take 2 tabs qid × 10 days.

> Rx: Famciclovir 500 mg.
> Disp: 21 tab.
> Sig: Take 1 tab tid × 7 days.

> Rx: Acyclovir 200 mg.
> Disp: 200 caps.
> Sig: Take 4 caps qid × 10 days.

> Rx: Systemic prednisone (see "Erosive Lichen Planus"). Systemic steroids may be used to treat severe postherpetic neuralgia and severe cases of zoster infection. Consultation with the patient's physician is recommended, especially in patients taking multiple medications or those who are immunosuppressed.

Tricyclic antidepressants may be indicated for postherpetic neuralgia pain.

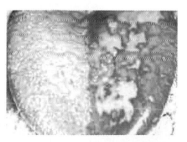

FIGURE 3-37
Lingual herpes zoster (shingles) affecting the unilateral third division of the trigeminal nerve.

Herpes Simplex

ETIOLOGY: A transmissible infection with herpes simplex virus, usually type I or, less commonly, type II. Primary herpetic gingivostomatitis is rare in the older patient, and typical lesions are usually of the recurrent type.

APPEARANCE: Clear vesicles develop intra- and extraorally and rupture within hours, forming shallow ulcers. Recurrent lesions typically occur on mucosa bound to bone and on the keratinized mucosa of the lips (herpes labialis; Figure 3-38). They can also occur on other mucosal surfaces in the immunocompromised patient (eg, those undergoing chemotherapy).

DIFFERENTIAL DIAGNOSIS: Traumatic lesion, primary and secondary syphilis, impetigo, aphthous ulcer

TREATMENT: Treatment is more effective if started in the prodromal stage or when lesions first appear.

Rx: Acyclovir ointment 5%.
Disp 15 g tube.
Sig: Apply to area q2h beginning with prodromal symptoms.

Rx: Penciclovir cream 1%.
Disp 15 g tube.
Sig: Apply to area q2h beginning with prodromal symptoms.

SYSTEMIC ANTIVIRAL DRUGS FOR IMMUNOCOMPROMISED PATIENTS Use acyclovir or valacyclovir HCl (see "Varicella Zoster [Herpes Zoster, Shingles]") at half of the recommended dose for herpes zoster.

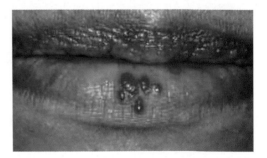

FIGURE 3-38
Recurrent herpes simplex
lesion on the lower lip (herpes
labialis).

LEUKOPLAKIC LESIONS OF THE SKIN AND ORAL MUCOSA

Senile or Actinic Keratosis

ETIOLOGY: Excessive exposure to sunlight, especially in fair-skinned people

APPEARANCE: Scaly lesions become firm and rough and eventually slough off lips and skin of the face, scalp, and other sun-exposed areas of the head and neck region.

DIFFERENTIAL DIAGNOSIS: Basal cell carcinoma, squamous cell carcinoma, keratoacanthoma

TREATMENT: Cryotherapy, chemical peels, topical chemotherapy ointments, retinoids, dermabrasion, laser or electrosurgical skin resurfacing, or surgical removal and biopsy of lesions owing to the potential for malignant transformation. Patient should use sunscreen with a sun protection factor > 15.

Leukoplakia

ETIOLOGY: Chronic irritation owing to smoking, alcohol, trauma, ill-fitting dentures, idiopathic

APPEARANCE: White nonremovable patch on any oral mucosal surface, most commonly on the buccal mucosa and tongue (Figure 3-39)

DIFFERENTIAL DIAGNOSIS: Hyperplastic candidosis, lichen planus, carcinoma in situ, squamous cell carcinoma, verrucous carcinoma

TREATMENT: Diagnostic biopsy owing to potential for malignant transformation, particularly of erythroleukoplakic areas. Surgical removal is the standard of care. Other treatments tested include topical retinoids and bleomycin. However, no treatment has been shown to be effective in preventing malignant transformation, and patients must be followed continuously, even after surgical removal.

FIGURE 3-39
Leukoplakia and mild dysplasia of the lateral border of the tongue.

NEOPLASMS OF THE ORAL MUCOSA

Squamous Cell Carcinoma

ETIOLOGY: Tobacco and alcohol use, chronic irritation, a diet low in fruits and vegetables, possible human papillomavirus. Suspected potentially premalignant lesions also include erosive lichen planus, leukoplakia, and dysplasia. Squamous cell carcinoma represents approximately 3% of all cancers but accounts for more than 90% of all oral and pharyngeal cancers. Five-year survival rates diminish with increased size of the lesion and regional metastasis to lymph nodes.

APPEARANCE: Squamous cell carcinoma consists of a red, white, or mixed red and white exophytic growth with poorly demarcated margins and constant erosions or ulcerations (Figure 3-40).

DIFFERENTIAL DIAGNOSIS: Leukoplakia, erythroplakia (Figure 3-41), traumatic lesions, erosive lichen planus, candidosis, carcinoma in situ, verrucous carcinoma, lymphoma

TREATMENT: Histologic diagnosis with biopsy. Refer to oncologic surgeon for surgical removal. More extensive lesions require head and neck radiation and possibly chemotherapy.

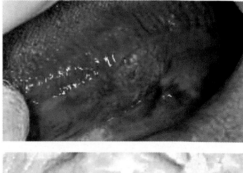

FIGURE 3-40
Stage I squamous cell carcinoma of the lateral border of the tongue in a 69-year-old female with no risk factors.

FIGURE 3-41
Palatal leukoplakia and erythroplakia with severe dysplasia.

Basal Cell Carcinoma

ETIOLOGY: Excessive exposure to sun

APPEARANCE: Ulcerative papule with rolled border on the lips, face, forehead, and ears. Lesions rarely metastasize but are locally invasive and destructive.

DIFFERENTIAL DIAGNOSIS: Keratoacanthoma, actinic keratosis, squamous cell carcinoma

TREATMENT: Surgical removal and histologic diagnosis. Refer to dermatologist or oncologic surgeon.

Lymphoma

ETIOLOGY: Neoplastic disorder of the lymph glands

APPEARANCE: Exophytic, ulcerated soft tissue lesions with poorly demarcated margins in mandible, maxilla, or palate (Figure 3-42). Mobile and rubbery pharyngeal and posterior tongue lymph nodes.

DIFFERENTIAL DIAGNOSIS: Squamous cell carcinoma, verrucous carcinoma, traumatic ulcer, erosive lichen planus

TREATMENT: Histologic diagnosis with biopsy. Refer to oncologic surgeon for removal; may require radiotherapy.

Salivary Gland Tumors

ETIOLOGY: Benign or malignant neoplasm of salivary glands. Parotid gland tumors may involve the facial nerve, resulting in facial paralysis.

APPEARANCE: New or recurrent swelling of major salivary glands. Minor salivary gland tumors have the clinical appearance of squamous cell carcinoma. Necrotizing sialometaplasia can affect the hard palate and resembles squamous cell carcinoma or an ulcer (Figure 3-43).

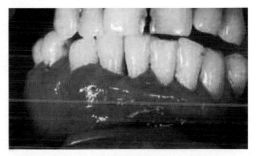

FIGURE 3-42
Lymphoma of gingival tissues.

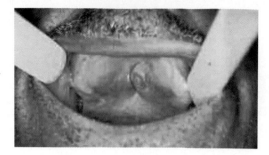

FIGURE 3-43
Necrotizing sialometaplasia of
the anterior hard palate.

DIFFERENTIAL DIAGNOSIS: Squamous cell carcinoma, traumatic ulcer, necrotizing sialometaplasia

TREATMENT: Histologic diagnosis with biopsy. Refer to oncologic surgeon for removal; may require radiotherapy.

PIGMENTED LESIONS OF THE ORAL MUCOSA

Malignant Melanoma

ETIOLOGY: Malignant transformation of melanin

APPEARANCE: Exophytic darkly pigmented lesions typically on the maxillary alveolar ridge or palate (Figure 3-44). May be associated with ulcerations.

DIFFERENTIAL DIAGNOSIS: Amalgam tattoo, nevus, oral melanocytic macule, hemangioma, hematoma, Kaposi's sarcoma

TREATMENT: Histologic diagnosis with biopsy. Refer to oncologic surgeon. Requires surgical removal and possible chemotherapy, radiation, and/or immunotherapy.

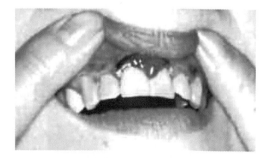

FIGURE 3-44
Melanoma of the anterior
gingival tissues.

Amalgam Tattoo

ETIOLOGY: Heavy metal within mucosa, usually secondary to amalgam

APPEARANCE: Pigmented lesion typically adjacent to teeth with metal restorations. Not exophytic; does not blanch with pressure. Dental radiographs confirm diagnosis.

DIFFERENTIAL DIAGNOSIS: Varix, nevus, oral melanocytic macule, hematoma, hemangioma, malignant melanoma, Kaposi's sarcoma

TREATMENT: Observe. Once a diagnosis is made, no treatment is required

Varix

ETIOLOGY: Tortuous veins in the ventral portion of the tongue, floor of the mouth, or labial or buccal mucosa

APPEARANCE: Exophytic, smooth-surfaced, purplish lesions (Figures 3-45 and 3-46)

DIFFERENTIAL DIAGNOSIS: Amalgam tattoo, hematoma, hemangioma, malignant melanoma

TREATMENT: Observe. Once a diagnosis is made, no treatment is required.

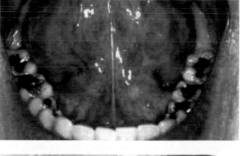

FIGURE 3-45
Lingual varicosities in an
82-year-old male.

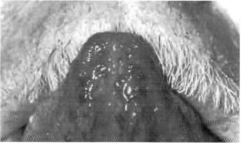

FIGURE 3-46
Lingual varicosities and
varices in a 74-year-old
female.

CONDITIONS AFFECTING THE TONGUE

Benign Migratory Glossitis (Geographic Tongue)

ETIOLOGY: Unknown. May be associated with psoriasis and Reiter's syndrome.

APPEARANCE: Changing pattern of erythematous patches on the tongue dorsum caused by atrophy of the filiform papillae. Lesions are surrounded by white hypertrophic papillae (Figure 3-47). Tongue may be sensitive to spicy foods.

DIFFERENTIAL DIAGNOSIS: Lichen planus, leukoplakia, traumatic lesion

TREATMENT: If symptomatic, use topical anesthetics (see "Oral Mucositis").

Median Rhomboid Glossitis (Central Papillary Atrophy of the Tongue)

ETIOLOGY: Possible candidosis

APPEARANCE: Smooth lobulated region on the dorsum of the tongue at the midline of the junction of the middle and posterior thirds of the tongue

DIFFERENTIAL DIAGNOSIS: Geographic tongue, chemical erosion

TREATMENT: If symptomatic, topical anesthetics (see "Oral Mucositis") and topical antifungals (see "Candidosis").

Hairy Tongue

ETIOLOGY: Antibiotics, tobacco, chlorhexidine, food debris, oral candidosis

APPEARANCE: Elongation and pigmentation of filiform papillae (Figures 3-48 and 3-49)

DIFFERENTIAL DIAGNOSIS: Hairy leukoplakia

TREATMENT: Proper oral hygiene and tongue brushing. If a fungal infection is suspected, perform a fungal culture and use topical antifungals (see "Candidosis").

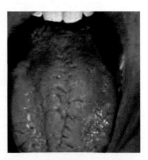

FIGURE 3-47
Geographic tongue (benign migratory glossitis).

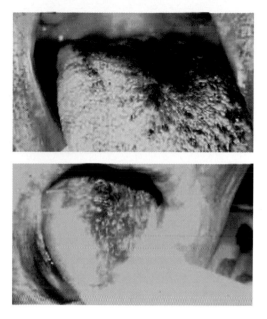

FIGURE 3-48
Black hairy tongue.

FIGURE 3-49
Brown hairy tongue.

Fissured Tongue

ETIOLOGY: Unknown

APPEARANCE: Numerous small furrows and fissures on the dorsum of the tongue. May be attributed to trauma, vitamin deficiencies, salivary gland dysfunction (see Figures 3-32, 3-33, 3-50, and 3-51).

DIFFERENTIAL DIAGNOSIS: Geographic tongue, nutritional deficiency

TREATMENT: Proper oral hygiene and tongue brushing. If symptomatic, use topical anesthetics (see "Oral Mucositis").

FIGURE 3-50
Fissured and coated tongue in a patient with poorly controlled hypothyroidism.

FIGURE 3-51
Fissured tongue in a patient
with salivary hypofunction
secondary to Sjögren's
syndrome.

Nutritional Deficiencies

ETIOLOGY: Vitamin B_1, B_2, B_6, and B_{12} and folic acid deficiency

APPEARANCE: Loss of filiform papillae produces a painful erythematous and granular-appearing tongue. Eventual papillae atrophy, leaving a smooth or bald tongue.

DIFFERENTIAL DIAGNOSIS: Severe salivary gland dysfunction. Determine serum levels of the nutrients to establish the diagnosis.

TREATMENT: Replacement therapy with appropriate nutrients

ADDITIONAL READINGS

Greenberg MS, Glick M. Burket's oral medicine. 10th ed. Hamilton (ON): BC Decker; 2003.

Siegel MA, Silverman S Jr, Sollecito TP. Treatment of common oral conditions. 6th ed. Hamilton (ON): BC Decker; 2006.

Silverman S Jr, Eversole LR, Truelove EL. Essentials of oral medicine. Hamilton (ON): BC Decker; 2001.

DENTAL TREATMENT GUIDELINES FOR COMMON GERIATRIC CONDITIONS

CANCER

Definition

Cancer is an uncontrollable growth of cells originating from normal tissues that can kill by local extension or metastasis. It is the second most common cause of death among adults aged 65+ years. Breast, prostate, lung, and colorectal cancer are the most common sites. Oral and pharyngeal cancers comprise approximately 2% of all cancers, with approximately 30,000 new cases each year in the United States. Approximately half of all oral and pharyngeal cancers occur in individuals aged 50+ years. Because the majority of oral and pharyngeal cancers are diagnosed in advanced stages, the average 5-year survival rate is only about 50%. The majority (90%) of head and neck cancers are epithelial squamous cell carcinomas, with the remainder cancers involving salivary glands, lymph nodes, and other tissues. There are also cancers that metastasize to the oral cavity and mandible from distant sites, and hematologic malignancies can occur in the mouth simultaneously with, or prior to, systemic signs and symptoms.

Etiology

Alcohol and tobacco use are the greatest risk factors for developing oral and pharyngeal cancers. Other risk factors include age, low intake of fruits and vegetables, human papillomavirus, and sun exposure for lip cancer. Long-standing leukoplakic lesions should be considered to be potentially premalignant and subjected to close follow-up, with biopsy of suspicious erythroplakic areas. Any non-healing oral ulcerative lesion that persists for 3 to 4 weeks, despite removal of any potential traumatic etiology, should be considered as a potential cancerous neoplasm and must be biopsied.

CLINICAL FINDINGS: SYSTEMIC
Extraoral

- The most common systemic sign of oral and pharyngeal cancer is enlarged head and neck lymph nodes.

Basal cell carcinomas
- This is the most common neoplasm of the facial skin, appearing as well-circumscribed, nonhealing, crusting, and ulcerative lesions.

Squamous cell carcinomas
- Head and neck squamous cell skin cancers are usually larger, crusting, and ulcerative lesions with poorly demarcated margins (see Figure 3-40 in Chapter 3, "Guide to Treatment of Common Oral Conditions").

Salivary gland cancers
- Tumors of the parotid, submandibular, and sublingual glands can be detected by the presence of nonresolving unilateral head and neck swellings.

Laryngeal cancer
- Hoarseness or other alteration of speech quality.

CLINICAL FINDINGS: ORAL
Most common sites
- The tongue, followed by the oropharynx, lip, floor of the mouth, gingiva, buccal mucosa, and hard palate.

The signs of oral cancer
- Signs can be very variable: ulcerative, leukoplakic, erythroplakic, crusting, or a combination of all four.
- Typically a lesion is exophytic, nonhealing, with poorly demarcated margins.
- Pain may or may not be present, whereas paresthesia is a sign of progressive disease.
- Metastatic lesions can appear in oral mucosal and bony tissues.
- Metastatic jaw lesions are usually painful, with accompanying swelling and numbness.
- They most commonly result from primary tumors of the breast, lung, renal, other bone, colon, and melanoma.

Hematologic malignancies
- These present with gingival (erythema, edema, hypertrophy, bleeding) and mucosal changes (purpura, pallor, nonhealing ulcers, secondary infections).

Medical Management

Treatment of cancers throughout the body typically includes surgery, radiotherapy, chemotherapy, or a combination of any of these three. The most common treatment for an oral-pharyngeal cancer is surgery with or without radiotherapy, depending upon the tumor stage. Smaller head and neck tumors with no or minimal lymph node involvement are treated with surgery alone, whereas more extensive cancers are surgically removed, followed by about 6 weeks of external beam radiotherapy. Nonsurgical head and neck tumors are treated with chemoradiation.

IMPLICATIONS FOR DENTAL/ORAL MEDICAL CARE

Overview

- Due to the immunosuppressive consequences of cancer chemotherapy, any patient receiving chemotherapy may encounter oral problems during or immediately after treatment.
- Head and neck surgery and radiotherapy can cause permanent consequences, and a pretreatment oral assessment is vital to help diminish peri- and post-treatment complications.
- Nonrestorable teeth and those with significant periodontal disease must be extracted, dental-alveolar infections resolved, and oral mucosal disorders stabilized prior to cancer treatment.
- Long-term follow-up is necessary to help maintain oral health and prevent radiotherapy-induced osteoradionecrosis, rampant caries, oral mucosal infections, xerostomia, trismus, and dysphagia.

CHEMOTHERAPY

Chemotherapy for any cancer can cause significant immunosuppression, which will predispose an individual to develop new and recurrent herpetic infections, oral candidiaosis (see Figure 3-21 in Chapter 3), gingivitis, and other oral infections.

Treatment of chemotherapy-induced oral diseases requires aggressive therapy, and systemic antiviral, antifungal, or antibiotic drugs should be initiated immediately.

Thrombocytopenia can produce spontaneous bleeding, and a platelet count of less than 50,000/mL requires medical consultation and possible platelet infusions prior to oral surgical procedures.

Neutropenia is likely, and an absolute neutrophil count (ANC) of less than 1,000/mL probably requires antibiotic prophylaxis before any necessary dental treatment. Severely neutropenic patients (ANC < 500/mL) with acute dental infections may require hospital admission and broad spectrum intravenous antibiotics until the neutrophil count is restored. Physician consultation is essential. Chlorhexidine oral rinses for gingivitis prevention are useful for the neutropenic patient.

Mucositis results from the direct cytotoxic effect of some chemotherapy agents on oral mucosa (see Figures 3-8 and 3-9 in Chapter 3). The mucosa becomes edematous, inflamed, and ulcerated with subsequent problems in swallowing and speaking. Pain varies considerably in severity and may be intensified by certain foods. The lips, cheeks, soft palate, and floor of the mouth are at greater risk of mucositis. Topical anesthetics, analgesics, and coating agents may provide pain relief. Severe symptoms usually resolve within 6 weeks following completion of therapy. Systemic analgesics (eg, acetaminophen, ibuprofen, naproxen) and narcotic analgesics may be needed. Sucking on ice chips may help prevent mucositis.

SURGERY

Head and neck surgery to remove neoplasms and lymph nodes can produce permanent parasthesias, facial deformities, oral pharyngeal–nasal defects, and trismus. Patients may experience difficulty with chewing and manipulation of a food bolus, swallowing, tasting, wearing removable prostheses, and speaking depending upon the site of cancer surgery. Additional surgeries may be required to further rehabilitate oral-facial function and aesthetics. Patients undergoing surgery to remove oral tumors or salivary glands must receive a presurgical oral evaluation to remove any potential complicating oral infections and to assist in the postsurgical rehabilitation process.

A rehabilitation plan should be discussed prior to surgery. Impressions may be needed for a surgical stent or temporary obturator when palatal/maxillary defects are anticipated. A presurgical facial moulage may facilitate fabrication of extraoral prostheses. If significant functional and aesthetic defects are anticipated, a consultation with a maxillofacial prosthodontist may be warranted.

RADIOTHERAPY

Therapeutic dosages of head and neck radiotherapy frequently exceed 6,000 cGy, which will cause acute and chronic problems to the oral-pharyngeal region. Prior to radiotherapy, an oral examination is necessary to assess oral health. Teeth that are nonrestorable and that have large dental-alveolar infections must be removed, foci of infection must be eliminated (advanced dental caries and periodontal disease, periradicular pathosis), and denture-related sores treated. Prescription strength daily topical fluorides are required to help prevent caries. Application may be via custom-made trays with 0.4% stannous fluoride or 1.1% sodium fluoride gel or as 5,000 ppm sodium fluoride prescription toothpaste. Professional application of fluorides at recalls is advised (see section on dental caries in Chapter 3).

Mucositis usually occurs after the second week of radiation therapy (see description above under "Chemotherapy" and section on oral mucositis in Chapter 3).

Permanent salivary gland dysfunction occurs when a salivary gland is in the field of radiotherapy approximately 2,500 cGy or more (Figures 3-31 and 3-32 in Chapter 3). If there is remaining salivary gland function after radiotherapy, saliva can be increased with masticatory (sugarless gums), gustatory (sugarless candies, mints), or pharmacologic (pilocarpine 5 mg three times a day [tid] 30 minutes before mealtime and qhs or cevimeline 30 mg tid 30 minutes before mealtime) stimulation. Salivary substitutes, frequent sips of sugarless beverages, and regular oral hygiene are helpful for xerostomia (see section on Salivary DYS-function and xerostomia in Chapter 3).

The risk of osteoradionecrosis is greater in the mandible versus the maxilla, increases with time, and increases with radiation dosages greater than 6,000 cGy. If extractions and/or alveolar preprosthetic surgery are required prior to radiotherapy, a minimum healing time of 2 to 3 weeks is necessary before the start of treatment. If extractions are required in the mandible and in the field of radiation therapy after the completion of radiotherapy, they should be performed within 6 months after the completion of radiotherapy. Hyperbaric oxygen (20 dives prior to surgery, 10 dives postsurgery), conservative surgical technique (minimal periosteal damage, primary closure), and pre-, peri-, and postsurgical antibiotics with good bone absorption (eg clindamycin, tetracycline) are recommended.

Construction of removable prostheses cannot start until all oral mucosal surfaces have completely healed following the completion of radiotherapy. This takes approximately 6 months. Denture-wearing patients must be reminded to visit the dentist at least yearly to evaluate all oral mucosal surfaces for any denture-related lesions.

CARDIOVASCULAR DISEASES

Syncope and Orthostatic Hypotension

Definition

Orthostatic hypotension is a symptomatic reduction of ≥ 20 mm Hg in systolic blood pressure or of ≥ 10 mm Hg in diastolic blood pressure on standing upright. It may lead to significant morbidity from syncope (fainting), falls, and their sequelae. It can occur in any elder with a normal or diseased cardiovascular system, and the incidence increases with age and institutionalization.

Etiology

In the elderly, decreased baroreceptor responsiveness, coupled with decreased arterial compliance, accounts for frequent orthostatic hypotension on sudden standing. Sudden standing causes pooling of blood in leg and trunk veins, decreasing venous return and cardiac output to create a transient drop in the blood pressure. The most common contributing factors to symptomatic orthostatic hypotension include hypovolemia, cardiac and autonomic nervous system disorders, and drugs that impair autonomic reflex mechanisms. The most common pathophysiologic basis for syncope is an acute decrease in cerebral blood flow (with resultant cerebral hypoxemia) secondary to decreased cardiac output generally due to arrhythmias.

CLINICAL FINDINGS: SYSTEMIC
- Faintness, light headedness, dizziness, confusion, or visual blurring is evidence of a mild to moderate reduction in cerebral blood flow and pending loss of consciousness.
- With syncope, the patient becomes unresponsive and loses postural tone.

CLINICAL FINDINGS: ORAL
- None.

Medical Management

If possible, identify and treat any underlying cause. Orthostatic hypotension due to hypovolemia or drug excess can be rapidly reversed by correcting these problems. If orthostatic hypotension is related to venous pooling in the legs, fitted elastic hose (support hose) may enhance the cardiac output and blood pressure on standing.

In the elderly, syncope may be due to the interaction of coexisting problems that may impair cardiovascular compensatory mechanisms. Elevation of the legs and lowering of the head helps reestablish cerebral perfusion to end the syncopal episode. Often, no further immediate treatment is needed unless required by the underlying cause. Repeated episodes in the elderly warrant cardiac evaluation. Bradyarrhythmias may require pacemaker implantation, and tachyarrhythmias require specific drug therapy. Management of volume depletion, hypoglycemia, anemia, electrolyte abnormality, or drug toxicity is standard. Other cardiac diseases may require treatment.

Implications for Dental/Oral Medical Care: Syncope and Orthostatic Hypotension
- Position patient in Trendelenburg position (head lower than heart and feet elevated) if patient begins to "feel faint."
- Return patient to upright position slowly.
- Support patient when getting out of chair.

Hypertension

Definition

A persistent elevation of systolic and/or diastolic arterial pressure. Diastolic blood pressure (BP) greater than or equal to 90 mm Hg and systolic greater than 140. Prehypertension is defined as diastolic of 80 to 89 or systolic of 120 to 139. Nearly 50% of persons over age 65 have chronic hypertension.

Etiology

In older patients, etiology is increased vascular resistance.

CLINICAL FINDINGS: SYSTEMIC
- Early cases are asymptomatic.
- Dizziness, flushed facies, headache, fatigue, epitaxis, and nervousness can be symptoms of uncontrolled hypertension.
- Complications in target organs include left ventricular failure, atherosclerotic heart disease, stroke or transient ischemic attacks, renal failure, peripheral arterial disease, and retinopathy.
- If a dentist detects elevated BP, the patient should be referred to the physician for diagnosis and treatment. Nearly one-third of individuals with hypertension are unaware of their disorder.

CLINICAL FINDINGS: ORAL

Antihypertensive medication side effects

- Dysgeusia
- Gingival hyperplasia
- Lichenoid reactions
- Salivary hypofunction
- Xerostomia

Medical Management

The treatment goal is to decrease BP to where cardiovascular risks are lower and drug side effects are minimal. Lifestyle modifications to lower BP are recommended for all patients with hypertension and prehypertension. They include maintaining a normal body weight, moderating alcohol intake (no more than 2 drinks per day for most men and 1 drink per day for most women), controlling dietary sodium ($\leq$ 2.3 g/day), exercising regularly, and consuming a diet rich in fruits, vegetables, and low-fat dairy products. Smoking cessation is recommended for overall cardiovascular risk reduction. Thiazide diuretics are commonly used as initial therapy for most patients with hypertension. Commonly used adjunctive pharmacologic agents include drugs from the following classes: beta blockers, calcium channel blockers, angiotensin receptor blockers, and angiotensin-converting enzyme (ACE) inhibitors. Treatment will lower the rate of strokes and heart failure.

IMPLICATIONS FOR DENTAL/ORAL MEDICAL CARE: HYPERTENSION

- No contraindication to treatment if BP is well controlled. Take BP before and after injection of local anesthetics.
- Encourage adherence to antihypertensive medication recommendations and lifestyle modifications.
- Defer elective dental treatment if BP is not controlled (over 180 systolic or over 110 diastolic). Refer immediately or within 1 week for physician evaluation.
- Stress/anxiety of dental appointment may bring on angina, myocardial infarction (MI), or stroke. Consider use of nitrous oxide/oxygen or other anxiolytics.
- Excessive use of epinephrine may increase BP. Minimize epinephrine use in local anesthetics and impregnated gingival retraction cord.
- Drug side effects may include orthostatic hypotension, confusion, depression, and oral signs/symptoms noted above.

Angina and MI

Definition

Angina pectoris is paroxysmal chest pain resulting from ischemic heart disease. MI is a sudden insufficiency of blood supply to the myocardium resulting in necrosis. MI is the most common cause of death in patients over 65.

Etiology

Angina and MI are clinical manifestations of ischemic heart disease, which is inadequate blood supply to the heart due to atherosclerosis. Risk factors include high cholesterol levels, hypertension, and smoking.

CLINICAL FINDINGS: SYSTEMIC
- Chest pain is the predominant symptom of MI in the elderly.
- The pain of MI typically is more severe and lasts longer than the pain of angina.
- Additional findings are dyspnea (shortness of breath), syncope, nausea/vomiting, and mental status changes.

CLINICAL FINDINGS: ORAL
- Pain during angina and/or MI can refer to the left mandible.

Medical Management

Drug therapy includes antianginals (nitrates, beta-blockers, calcium channel blockers), antilipidemics. In more severe cases, cardiac catheterization with balloon angioplasty and vascular stents or coronary artery bypass graft surgery may be required. The elderly patient with acute MI derives significant benefit from fibrinolytic-based reperfusion, such as tissue plasminogen activator (t-PA), if given within 3 hours of symptom onset. Post MI patients are typically placed on antithrombotic medication, most commonly a platelet inhibitor.

IMPLICATIONS FOR DENTAL/ORAL MEDICAL CARE: ANGINA AND MI
- Stress/anxiety of dental appointment may bring on angina or MI.
- Short, low-stress appointments are suggested. Consider use of anxiolytics.
- Obtain effective anesthesia; monitor use of epinephrine.
- Terminate appointment if patient becomes fatigued or short of breath.
- Drug side effects may include orthostatic hypotension, sedation, confusion, salivary dysfunction, gingival enlargement, and prolonged postsurgical bleeding.
- Physician consultation is recommended for any patient with a history of MI.
- Consider deferring elective dental care within the first 2 months following a MI. Elective care should be safe 2 months after an MI if the patient's cardiac status is stable and the patient is being followed by a medical provider.
- If chest pain develops during a dental procedure, the procedure should be stopped and sublingual nitroglycerin given. Monitor vital signs. Up to 3 tablets may be given in 15 minutes. If pain persists, call for emergency medical care.

Bacterial Endocarditis

Definition

Inflammation/infection of the cardiac valves and the endocardium, usually caused by streptococcal species (eg viridans streptococci) and less often by *Staphylococcus aureus, Staphylococcus epidermidis,* and fastidious *Haemophilus* sp.

Etiology

Structural defects of cardiac valves or altered blood flow around valve leaflets predispose to bacterial deposition. Some dental and surgical procedures cause transient bacteremias. Infective endocarditis occurs most often on the left side, involving the mitral, aortic, tricuspid, and pulmonic valves (in descending order of frequency). In elderly patients, the predominant causes of valvular heart disease that may lead to infective endocarditis are degenerative calcification (such as aortic and mitral valve stenosis), myxomatous degeneration, and papillary muscle dysfunction.

CLINICAL FINDINGS: SYSTEMIC
- Malaise, night sweats, fatigability, pallor
- Chills and arthralgias
- Heart murmur with valvular insufficiency
- Fever (acute and high fever in acute endocarditis, low-grade fever in subacute endocarditis)
- Petechiae over the upper trunk, conjunctiva, mucous membranes, and distal extremities
- Splinter hemorrhages under the nails, hemorrhagic retinal lesions
- Emboli may produce stroke, MI, flank pain and hematuria, abdominal pain, or acute arterial insufficiency in an extremity
- With prolonged infection, splenomegaly or clubbing of the fingers and toes may also be present

CLINICAL FINDINGS: ORAL
- None known

Medical Management

Antibiotics, primarily intravenous penicillin G for susceptible strains. Cardiac valve surgery (débridement and/or replacement of the valve) is frequently required to eradicate infection that is uncontrolled medically, particularly in early-onset prosthetic valve endocarditis.

IMPLICATIONS FOR DENTAL/ORAL MEDICAL CARE: BACTERIAL ENDOCARDITIS

- Patients need to be reminded that they must maintain the best possible oral health to reduce the further risk of bacteremia. The importance of effective daily oral hygiene practices should be emphasized.
- Although most cases of endocarditis are not attributable to an invasive dental procedure, the American Heart Association recommendations for the prevention of bacterial endocarditis most recently updated in 1997 should be followed (Tables 4-1 to 4-3).
- Cardiac conditions are categorized into high-, moderate-, and negligible-risk categories based on potential outcome if endocarditis develops.
- Dental procedures are either recommended or not recommended for coverage based on presumptive bacteremia-inducing potential.
- Post–oral procedure antibiotics are no longer necessary.

TABLE 4-1. CARDIAC CONDITIONS ASSOCIATED WITH ENDOCARDITIS

Endocarditis Prophylaxis Recommended	*Endocarditis Prophylaxis Not Recommended*
High-Risk Category	Negligible-Risk Category (no greater risk than the general population)
• Prosthetic heart valves, including bioprosthetic and homograft valves	• Isolated secundum atrial septal defect
• Previous bacterial endocarditis	• Surgical repair of atrial septal defect, ventricular septal defect, or patent ductus arteriosus (without residua beyond 6 months)
• Complex cyanotic congenital heart disease (eg single ventricle states, transposition of the great arteries, tetralogy of Fallot)	
• Surgically constructed systemic pulmonary shunts or conduits	• Previous coronary artery bypass graft surgery
	• Mitral valve prolapse without valvular regurgitation
Moderate-Risk Category	• Physiologic, functional, or innocent heart murmurs
• Most other congenital cardiac malformations	
• Acquired valvular dysfunction (eg, rheumatic heart disease)	• Previous Kawasaki disease or rheumatic fever without valvular dysfunction
• Hypertrophic cardiomyopathy	• Cardiac pacemakers (intravascular and epicardial) and implanted defibrillators
• Mitral valve prolapse with valvular regurgitation and/or thickened leaflets	

TABLE 4-2. DENTAL PROCEDURES AND ENDOCARDITIS PROPHYLAXIS

Endocarditis Prophylaxis Recommended	Endocarditis Prophylaxis Not Recommended
Dental extractions	Restorative dentistry (operative and prosthodontic) with or without retraction cord*
Periodontal procedures including surgery, scaling and root planing, probing, and recall maintenance	Local anesthetic injections (nonintraligamentary)
Dental implant placement and reimplantation of avulsed teeth	Intracanal endodontic treatment; post placement and build-up
Endodontic instrumentation or surgery only beyond the apex	Placement of rubber dams
Subgingival placements of antibiotic fibers or strips	Postoperative suture removal
Intraligamentary local anesthetic injections	Placement of removable prosthodontic or orthodontic appliances
Prophylactic cleaning of teeth or implants where bleeding is anticipated	Taking of oral impressions
	Fluoride treatments
	Taking of oral radiographs

*Clinical judgment may indicate antibiotic use in selected circumstances that may create significant bleeding.

TABLE 4-3. PROPHYLACTIC REGIMEN FOR DENTAL AND ORAL PROCEDURES

Standard General Prophylaxis	Unable to Take Oral Medications
Amoxicillin 2.0 g 1 hour before procedure	Ampicillin 2.0 g IM or IV within 30 minutes before procedure

Allergic to Penicillin	Allergic to Penicillin and Unable to Take Oral Medications
Clindamycin 600 mg 1 hour before procedure or *cephalexin or cefadroxil 2.0 g 1 hour before procedure or azithromycin or clarithromycin 500 mg 1 hour before procedure	Clindamycin 600 mg IV within 30 min before procedure or *cefazolin 1.0 g IM or IV within 30 minutes before procedure

*Cephalosporins should not be used in individuals with immediate-type hypersensitivity reaction (urticaria, angioedema, or anaphylaxis) to penicillin.

IM= intramuscular; IV = intravenous.

Congestive Heart Failure

Definition

An advanced stage of impaired heart function with edema and congestion of pulmonary and systemic venous circulation. Cardiac output is insufficient to meet physiologic demands.

Etiology

Underlying cardiac problem such as atrial fibrillation, valvular disease, coronary artery disease, or hypertension. Any condition that places an additional burden on the cardiovascular system, such as anemia, MI, or infection, can precipitate heart failure in a patient with heart disease.

CLINICAL FINDINGS: SYSTEMIC
All adults
- Cyanosis
- Dyspnea
- Fatigue
- Orthopnea
- Peripheral edema

Older adults (in addition to above finding)
- Confusion
- Disorientation
- Failure to thrive
- Somnolence
- Weakness

CLINICAL FINDINGS: ORAL
- Drug side effects may include salivary hypofunction, xerostomia, orthostatic hypotension, nausea and vomiting.

Medical Management

The goal is an increased quality of life and improved survival. Measures include attempts to identify and manage exacerbating factors or disorders, including dietary (eg, sodium) indiscretion, drug nonadherence, and inadequate BP control. Control of hyperlipidemia and diabetes, smoking and alcohol cessation, and light to moderate physical activity are useful. Drugs include diuretics, ACE inhibitors, angiotensin II receptor blockers, and digoxin. Patients with atrial fibrillation may also be taking coumadin.

IMPLICATIONS FOR DENTAL/ORAL MEDICAL CARE: CONGESTIVE HEART FAILURE
- Physician consultation is recommended, especially in severely ill patients because survival is poor.

- Stress increases workload on the heart and should be avoided; short low-stress appointments are suggested.
- Dental care can generally be provided using precautions appropriate for the patient's underlying cardiac condition.
- Patients are prone to pulmonary edema if supine position is used too long; therefore, use a semi-upright position.
- Pulmonary edema results in impaired gas exchange. Signs/symptoms include acute dyspnea, anxiety, frothy productive cough, cyanosis. Should this occur, administer oxygen, keep the patient upright, and call for emergency medical services.

CEREBROVASCULAR DISEASES

Cerebrovascular Accident Stroke Syndrome

Definition
A heterogeneous category of illnesses that describes brain injury due to acute vascular lesions such as hemorrhage, embolism, thrombosis, and rupturing aneurysm. With an incidence of 750,000 cases/year, it is sudden in onset and is the third leading cause of death in the United States. Furthermore, the incidence of stroke and death from stroke increases with age, especially after 65 years. About 72% of persons who have a stroke in a given year are age 65+, and > 88% of persons who die of stroke are age 65+.

Etiology
Approximately 80% of strokes are associated with the development of atherosclerosis leading to cerebral ischemia and infarction. The remaining 20% of cases are caused by subarachnoid hemorrhage. Nonhemorrhagic cerebrovascular accident (CVA) has gradual onset, whereas hemorrhagic CVA has rapid onset and intense signs and symptoms. The interruption/cessation of blood flow to the nerve cells in the brain may result in cell death and subsequent loss of neuromotor function. Atrial fibrillation, high BP, left ventricular hypertrophy, diabetes, cigarette smoking, hypercholesterolemia, and aging are significant risks for stroke.

CLINICAL FINDINGS: SYSTEMIC
The clinical presentation varies based on the duration, location, and severity of injury to the brain.
- Weakness or numbness of the contralateral limbs and the face
- Aphasia
- Transient monocular blindness, diplopia, and blurred vision
- Dizziness, vertigo
- Memory loss
- Staggering gait

Clinical Findings: Oral
- Cranial nerve defects involving nerves V, VII, IX, and X

Medical Management of Acute-Onset Cerebrovascular Event

Thrombolysis is an option when patients can be treated soon after the onset of symptoms of brain ischemia and when an arterial occlusion is identified by diagnostic tests (computed tomography or magnetic resonance imaging-guided angiography, extracranial and transcranial ultrasonography, or catheterization angiography) before extensive brain infarction has occurred. Intravenous thrombolysis is used when intracranial branch arteries are occluded, but it is ineffective for carotid artery occlusion. Fibrinolytic agents (t-PA, streptokinase, urokinase) have also been used in the treatment of elderly patients with ischemic stroke following careful screening, including a scan of the brain, to exclude hemorrhagic stroke.

Transient Ischemic Attack or "Minor Stroke"

Definition

Sudden but reversible neurologic deficit that lasts from a few minutes to 24 hours. The majority last less than 5 minutes. Transient ischemic attack (TIA) is a warning sign of stroke, with at least one-third of people with one or more TIAs going on to have strokes.

Etiology

Temporary disturbance in blood supply to a localized area of the brain.

Clinical Findings: Systemic
- Muscle weakness
- Tingling, numbness of the face, arm, and/or leg
- Speech disturbance

Clinical Findings: Oral
- Disturbed orofacial sensations
- Dysphagia
- Slurred speech

Completed Stroke

Definition

A clinically stabilized or improving condition in which maximal deficit has been acquired as a result of a CVA. There are about 2 million stroke survivors in the United States.

Etiology

CVA leaving residual defects.

CLINICAL FINDINGS: SYSTEMIC

General

- Agnosia
- Aphasia
- Apraxia
- Diminished gag
- Dysarthria
- Hemiplegia
- Language and speech disorders
- Paresis

Right hemiplegics (left brain damage)

- Anxiety and nervousness
- Decreased auditory memory
- Language problems
- Slow, cautious, disorganized behavior

Left hemiplegics (right brain damage)

- Impulsive behavior
- Memory deficits
- Spatial-perceptual deficits
- Thought impairment
- Visual fields diminished
- Visual memory decreased

CLINICAL FINDINGS: ORAL

- Weak palate, flaccid tongue, unilateral paralysis of orofacial musculature
- Slurred speech
- Dysphagia
- Poor oral hygiene involving the affected side (Figure 4-1)

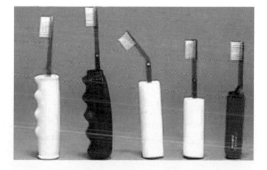

FIGURE 4-1
Toothbrushes attached to a hand grip can be useful for patients with compromised manual dexterity.

Medical Management

The goal is to identify risk factors and then attempt to reduce and/or eliminate as many as possible. Anticoagulant/antiplatelet therapy (eg, clopidogrel, warfarin, aspirin, dipyridamole, and the new inhibitors of the platelet glycoprotein IIb/IIIa complex and its binding to fibrinogen, including abciximab, eptifibatide, lamifiban, and tirofiban), carotid endarterectomy, and carotid angioplasty often with stenting are methods of prevention in some patients with TIA. Treatment goals also include preventing further thrombosis or hemorrhage and to rehabilitate using physiotherapy and speech therapy (if needed).

IMPLICATIONS FOR DENTAL/ORAL MEDICAL CARE: CEREBROVASCULAR DISEASES

- Identify risk factors and encourage control.
- Beware of presence of calcified atherosclerotic plaques in carotid arteries of elderly as a risk factor, easily captured by panoramic radiographs.
- Defer oral care until stabilized. Defer elective surgical procedures until 6 months post stroke.
- Evaluate patient's bleeding function. Consult physician if prothrombin (PT) > 2.0 to 2.5 times normal or international normalized ratio (INR) > 3.0 to 3.5 or if patient is receiving intravenous heparin.
- Minimize use of vasoconstrictor in anesthetic, and no epinephrine should be used in retraction cord.
- Keep appointments short.
- Monitor BP.
- Have hemostatic agents available.
- Use effective communication techniques (ie, simple, brief questions; no "baby talk"; simple drawing; do not wear a mask while talking with patient).
- Modify oral hygiene aids if needed (see Figure 4-1).

ENDOCRINE DISEASES

Diabetes Mellitus

Definition

Syndrome of abnormal carbohydrate, fat, and protein metabolism resulting in multiple acute and chronic complications as a result of the absolute or relative lack of insulin.

Type I diabetes mellitus (DM) (formerly known as insulin-dependent diabetes mellitus)
- Onset typically occurs before 40 years of age
- Considered an autoimmune process
- Patients are dependent on insulin for life

Type II diabetes mellitus (formerly known as non–insulin-dependent diabetes mellitus)
- Onset typically occurs after age 40 but can occur at any age
- Managed by diet therapy and/or oral hypoglycemics
- Insulin is used only if patients are refractory to other therapy

Secondary diabetes results from another disease or treatment
- Drug therapy with corticosteroids and thiazide diuretics
- Hyperpituitarism, hyperthyroidism, hyperadrenalism, and pancreatic disease have been associated with elevated glucose levels

This section focuses on type II diabetes because type I is rare in elderly and 25% of all type II diabetics are over 85 years. It is thought that 50% of adults with diabetes in the United States are undiagnosed.

Etiology

Type II: An alteration in target tissue sensitivity to insulin or abnormalities in the production of insulin.

CLINICAL FINDINGS: SYSTEMIC
Cardiac/vascular
- Poor wound healing
- Atherosclerosis
- Retinopathy

Genitourinary
- Vaginitis

Infectious
- Recurrent infections

Dermatologic, immunologic, allergic
- Pruritis

Metabolic
- Obesity (varies from 30–100% based on ethnicity)
- Fruity breath odor (serum glucose > 300 mg/dL)

Neurologic
- Peripheral neuropathy
- Blurred vision
- Mental confusion (serum glucose < 50–70 mg/dL)
- Neuromuscular
- Convulsions (serum glucose < 40 mg/dL)
- Muscle weakness
- Lethargy

CLINICAL FINDINGS: ORAL

Dental tissues
* Dental caries

Oral mucosa
* Burning tongue
* Fungal infections (Figures 3-19 and 3-22 in Chapter 3)
* Poor wound healing

Periodontal and gingival tissues
* Gingivitis (Figure 3-2 in Chapter 3)
* Periodontitis

Salivary glands
* Xerostomia
* Salivary hypofunction
* Sialadenosis

Medical Management

The goals of treatment are to (1) normalize blood glucose levels; (2) prevent acute complications and eliminate symptoms; (3) maintain ideal body weight; and (4) prevent or minimize chronic complications. Note, however, that most clinicians will accept higher glucose levels when treating elderly diabetics because they are particularly prone to complications of hypoglycemia. Oral hypoglycemic medications (sulfonylureas) depend on functioning pancreatic B cells to stimulate insulin secretion and are therefore used for treatment of non–insulin dependent diabetes mellitus (NIDDM). Insulin is required for type I diabetics as well as type II diabetics who do not respond to diet therapy alone or in diet combination with oral hypoglycemics.

Home glucose monitoring is recommended, but many elderly either cannot afford it or cannot use the instrumentation without assistance. Monitoring urine sugar can give useful information but is associated with a time-lag of several hours; some elderly can have difficulty reading the "colorimetric" scales due to age-related changes in color vision.

Measurement of glycosylated hemoglobin should be interpreted with caution in the elderly because studies have reported elevated levels despite the absence of glucose intolerance. This may be attributed to factors other than glucose that can alter levels of glycosylated hemoglobin (chronic blood loss, presence of abnormal hemoglobins, thalassemia, chronic renal failure, dialysis, splenectomy, elevated triglycerides).

IMPLICATIONS FOR DENTAL/ORAL MEDICAL CARE: DIABETES MELLITUS
- Dental therapy should not interfere with the medical control of DM, but if it does, modification of medical/diet therapy may be made in consultation with the physician.
- Large amounts of epinephrine and corticosteroids can antagonize the effects of insulin and result in hyperglycemia.
- Medications with hypoglycemic activity include aspirin, sulfa antibiotics, and antidepressants.
- The poorly controlled patient with DM is at risk of developing oral complications due to susceptibility to infection and its sequelae and will likely require supplemental antibiotics.
- Minimize stress and monitor closely oral-facial infections.

Hypothyroidism

Definition

Insufficient secretion by the thyroid gland due to primary disease of the thyroid, lack of pituitary thyroid-stimulating hormone (TSH), or lack of hypothalamic thyroid-releasing hormone. True end-organ insensitivity to normal thyroid hormone is rare. Hypothyroidism is common in the elderly, with a prevalence ranging from 1 to 10%.

Etiology

Autoimmune atrophy, Hashimoto's thyroiditis, previous thyroid surgery, previous radioactive iodine therapy, recent discontinuation of thyroid hormone.

CLINICAL FINDINGS: SYSTEMIC
Cardiac
- Congestive heart failure

Dermatologic
- Alopecia
- Atrophic epidermis
- Coarse hair
- Grooved nails
- Hyperkeratosis of stratum corneum
- Loss of lateral third of eyebrows

Endocrine
- Cold intolerance

Gastrointestinal
- Constipation

Neuromuscular
- Lethargy

Psychiatric
- Altered mental status
- Debilitation and apathy

Pulmonary
- Alveolar hypoventilation
- Occult pulmonary infections

CLINICAL FINDINGS: ORAL AND PERIORAL
Extraoral findings
- Puffy face
- Enlarged lips

Oral mucosa
- Thickened tongue (Figure 3-50 in Chapter 3)

Periodontal and gingival tissues
- Gingival edema and gingivitis (Figure 3-1 in Chapter 3)

Medical Management

Replacement of thyroid hormone. Increased age is associated with an increased half-life of thyroxin

IMPLICATIONS FOR DENTAL/ORAL MEDICAL CARE: HYPOTHYROIDISM
- There is no contraindication to routine dental treatment in the well-managed hypothyroid patient.
- Edematous oral tissues generally resolve with successful treatment of hypothyroidism.
- Myxedema is the severest form of hypothyroidism and can occur in untreated or uncontrolled hypothyroidism. It is precipitated by stress, extremely cold weather, infection, and the use of central nervous system (CNS) depressants.
- Increased response to CNS depressants (narcotic analgesics, sedatives) may occur in hypothyroidism.

Hyperthyroidism

Definition

A constellation of symptoms associated with excessive thyroid hormone. Elderly men and women are affected equally, in contrast to the preponderance of younger females who develop the disease. There is a sevenfold greater prevalence of hyperthyroidism among adults aged 60+ years compared with persons younger than age 60.

Etiology

Toxic nodular goiter is the most common cause of hyperthyroidism in the elderly. Graves' disease, an autoimmune disorder, may occur at any age but usually occurs in adults aged 20 to 40 years. Other causes include iodine-induced hyperthyroidism, subacute thyroiditis (secondary to viral infection or interleuki-2 therapy), thyrotoxicosis factitia (ingestion of excessive thyroid hormone), toxic adenomas, and tumors that secrete β–human chorionic gonadotropin (hCG structurally resembles TSH).

CLINICAL FINDINGS: SYSTEMIC
Cardiac
- Tachycardia

Endocrine
- Goiter
- Heat intolerance

Gastrointestinal
- Diarrhea
- Vomiting
- Weight loss

Neuromuscular
- Fine tremor (may be mistaken as senile tremor)
- Muscle wasting

Ophthalmic
- Exophthalmia

Psychiatric
- Anorexia
- Depression
- Nervousness

CLINICAL FINDINGS: ORAL
Oral Motor
- Increased tremor of the tongue may be present

Medical Management

Surgery, antithyroid medication, radioactive iodine 131 therapy. Propranolol is used to reduce associated sympathomimetic activity.

IMPLICATIONS FOR DENTAL/ORAL MEDICAL CARE: HYPERTHYROIDISM
- Elective dental care is not indicated for the patient with uncontrolled hyperthyroidism because the patient is very susceptible to the effects of epinephrine.
- Use <u>caution</u> with local anesthetics containing epinephrine.
- Do <u>not</u> use gingival retraction cord containing epinephrine.
- Administered medications may be metabolized more rapidly because body temperature and hepatic metabolism can be elevated.
- Agranulocytosis is a rare effect of thioureas used to treat hyperthyroidism.

HEMATOLOGIC DISEASES

Decreased White Blood Cell Disorders (Leukopenias)

Definition

Decreased absolute number of white blood cells (WBCs) (leukopenia; WBC count < 4,000 cells/mm^3) that is divided largely into disorders of the two predominant components of the differential (eg, neutrophils and lymphocytes).

Neutropenia

Definition

Absolute neutrophil count (ANC) < 2,000 cells/mm^3; considered to be moderate if ANC 500–1,000 or severe if ANC < 500.

Etiology

Drug toxicity (eg, phenothiazines, anticonvulsants, and antibiotics, including penicillins and other beta-lactams), cancer chemotherapy, and medical problems (eg, leukemia, aplastic anemia, metastatic cancer).

CLINICAL FINDINGS: SYSTEMIC
- Acute bacterial infections from *Staphylococcus aureus* or gram-negative bacilli, acute pharyngitis, lymphadenopathy, and mucosal ulcers.
- Common sites of infection are lungs, urinary tract, skin, rectum, and mouth.
- Fever is the most common sign because localized clinical signs of infection (suppuration, swelling, redness) may be suppressed.

CLINICAL FINDINGS: ORAL
- Oral mucosal ulcerations
- Exacerbated dental-alveolar infections
- Severe forms of gingivitis and periodontitis

Medical Management

Treat the underlying cause, remove any suspected drugs, and use of drugs (e.g., granulocyte colony-stimulating factor filgrastim).

IMPLICATIONS FOR DENTAL/ORAL MEDICAL CARE: NEUTROPENIA
- Signs and symptoms of infection may be suppressed.
- Oral ulceration may be a presenting sign. Lesions are characteristically necrotic and lack surrounding inflammation.
- Patients with severe neutropenia are highly susceptible to bacterial infections, making dental treatment inducing bacteremia a risky procedure.

- Antibiotic prophylaxis should be used prior to invasive dental procedures when the ANC < 500. For patients with ANC < 500 due to cytotoxic chemotherapy, physician consultation is warranted prior to treatment.

Lymphopenia

Definition
Lymphocyte count < 1,500 cells/mm^3

Etiology
Medical problems (eg, human immunodeficiency virus infection, renal failure), cancer chemotherapy, and medications (immunosuppressive drugs, corticosteroids).

CLINICAL FINDINGS: SYSTEMIC
- Few
- Possible increased incidence of fungal and viral infections

CLINICAL FINDINGS: ORAL
- Few
- Possible increased incidence of candidosis and herpes simplex infections

Medical Management
Treat the underlying cause and remove any suspected drug.

IMPLICATIONS FOR DENTAL/ORAL MEDICAL CARE: LYMPHOPENIA
- Lymphopenia predisposes the patient to fungal infections (eg, oral candidosis and deep fungal infections) and viral infections (eg, recurrent herpes infections).
- Treat aggressively with appropriate antimicrobial therapy.

Leukemia

Definition
Cancer of the WBCs, in either acute or chronic forms, and lymphoid or myeloid cell proliferation. Chronic lymphocytic is the most common form in adults and has slower onset of symptoms and better prognosis than acute leukemia.

Etiology
Unknown, however possible, increased risk with exposure to large doses of ionizing radiation, certain chemicals (eg, benzene, previous chemotherapy), and viruses (eg, human T-cell lymphotropic virus [HTLV]-I or HTLV-II).

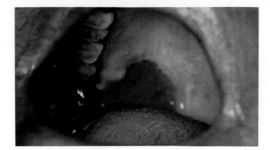

FIGURE 4-2
Intraoral ecchymosis in a
65-year-old-black female with
acute myelogenous leukemia
and a platelet count of 9,000.

CLINICAL FINDINGS: SYSTEMIC
Constitutional
• Fever, weakness

Skin and mucosa
• Pallor, bleeding, ecchymoses, and petechiae (Figure 4-2)

Lymphatic/organ enlargement
• Lymphadenopathy, enlarged tonsils, splenomegaly

Hematologic
• Significantly increased WBC counts, with atypical, immature, poorly functioning forms
• Decreased platelet count
• Reduced red blood cell counts

CLINICAL FINDINGS: ORAL
Oral mucosa
• Ulcerations

Infections
• Mucosal bleeding, ecchymoses, and petechiae

Gingival and periodontal tissues
• Gingival enlargements due to leukemic infiltrates
• Gingival and mucosal bleeding, ecchymoses, and petechiae

Medical Management

Combination of cytotoxic chemotherapy and supportive blood product transfusions (eg, platelets), bone marrow transplant in selected cases.

IMPLICATIONS FOR DENTAL/ORAL MEDICAL CARE: LEUKEMIA
• Gingival bleeding may require platelet transfusion or local hemostatic measures.
• Gingival enlargements will resolve with effective chemotherapy.
• Oral ulcerations and chemotherapy-induced mucositis may require systemic pain management or local anesthetic mouth rinses (see section on ulcerative lesions of the oral mucosa).

- Chlorhexidine oral rinse is effective for gingivitis control and reduction in systemic seeding of oral bacteria via oral ulcerations.
- Odontogenic infection requires prompt treatment.
- Candidosis and herpetic lesions may develop and require immediate treatment.
- Invasive dental treatments should be scheduled during chemotherapy to avoid periods of severe neutropenia and thrombocytopenia.

Multiple Myeloma

Definition
Plasma cell malignancy resulting from a malignant proliferation of plasma and myeloma cells, primarily in the bone marrow.

Etiology
Unknown. Genetic factors, radiation exposure, age-related decrease in cell-mediated immunity, chronic antigenic stimulation from systemic inflammatory disease, asbestos exposure, and viral illnesses (eg, human herpesvirus 6) have been suggested as possible etiologic factors. There are approximately 10,000 new cases per year, with no gender predilection. Multiple myeloma usually occurs in people > 50 years, and incidence increases with age.

CLINICAL FINDINGS: SYSTEMIC
Constitutional
- Weakness, easy fatigability
- Weight loss

Skeletal
- Bone pain
- Punched-out lesions on skeletal radiographs
- Pathologic fractures
- Generalized osteoporosis

Hematologic
- Anemia, leukopenia, thrombocytopenia, decreased plasma immunoglobulins, hypercalcemia

Organ involvement
- Renal failure

CLINICAL FINDINGS: ORAL
- Single or multiple "punched-out" or mottled radiolucent lesions on dental/facial radiographs
- Soft tissue plasma cell tumors

Medical Management

Combination chemotherapy. In elderly persons, the most common regimens are intermittent melphalan with prednisone or low-dose continuous melphalan.

IMPLICATIONS FOR DENTAL/ORAL MEDICAL CARE: MULTIPLE MYELOMA

- A bleeding diathesis, partially due to thrombocytopenia and disturbances of the coagulation cascade, is present in 15% of patients.
- Presurgical assessment of coagulation is warranted.
- The ability to control infections may be impaired and antibiotic therapy may be indicated for surgical procedures.
- Treatment with high dose bisphosphonates may place patients at risk for osteonecrosis.

Decreased Red Blood Cell Disorders (Anemias)

Definition

Decreased circulating hemoglobin (Hb) carrying erythrocytes leads to diminished tissue oxygenation. Males: Hb < 14 g/dL. Females: Hb < 12 g/dL. In healthy older persons, the Hb levels may be a little lower, but anemia is not a sign of old age. The Hb level is, however, an indicator of ill health in older people. Table 4-4 outlines the major types of anemias.

TABLE 4-4. MAJOR TYPES OF AMEMIAS	
Microcytic (iron deficiency anemia)	• Due to inadequate intake, impaired absorption, or chronic gastrointestinal blood loss
Macrocytic	• Normoblastic: young red cell population, alcoholism, hypothyroidism, drugs, neoplasia, leukemic and preleukemic syndromes, aplastic and hypoplastic anemia, liver disease, chronic obstructive airway disease • Megaloblastic (pernicious anemia): due to cobalamin (B12) deficiency, folate deficiency, drugs
Hemolytic	• Sickle cell disease • Autoimmune disease
Normocytic and anemias of chronic disease	• The most common of all anemias in the elderly • Usually mild and not progressive and frequently associated with infection, malignancy, collagen diseases, and after certain injuries to soft tissue and bone

CLINICAL FINDINGS: SYSTEMIC
Skin and mucosa
- Pallor

Cardiovascular
- Tachycardia
- Breathlessness
- Peripheral edema

Cerebrovascular
- Dizziness, apathy, confusion
- Depression leading to self-neglect
- Paresthesias

Gastrointestinal
- Atrophic gastritis

CLINICAL FINDINGS: ORAL
Oral mucosa
- Angular stomatitis
- Atrophic glossitis
- Mucosal pallor

Medical Management
a. Microcytic: oral (ferrous sulfate) and parenteral (iron dextran) iron
b. Macrocytic: normoblastic (treat primary cause); megaloblastic (parenteral hydroxocobalamin)
c. Hemolytic and normocytic: treat primary condition

IMPLICATIONS FOR DENTAL/ORAL MEDICAL CARE: ANEMIAS
- Macrocytic anemia results in epithelial changes causing the tongue to be red, sore, and smooth.
- Acute blood loss from oral surgical procedures can exacerbate preexisting anemia.
- Hb concentration of 7.0 g/dL or more is recommended for adequate oxygen carrying capacity to support general anesthesia when required for dental treatment.
- Avoid respiratory depressing drugs with Hb < 10 g/dL.
- Bone marrow hyperplasia may result in diffuse radiolucency of bone on dental radiographs.

Decreased Platelet Disorders (Thrombocytopenia)

Definition
Platelet count < 140,000/mm^3.

Etiology

Production defects such as marrow injury (eg, drugs, irradiation), marrow failure (eg, aplastic anemia), and marrow invasion (eg, carcinoma, leukemia); sequestration due to splenomegaly; and accelerated destruction (due to drugs, autoimmune disease, disseminated intravascular coagulation, viral infections, or hemorrhage).

CLINICAL FINDINGS: SYSTEMIC
Findings depend upon disease severity

Skin and mucosa
- Easy bruising
- Ecchymosis of the skin and mucosa

Nasal
- Epistaxis

Genitourinary
- Hematuria

Life-threatening hemorrhage
- Spontaneous hemorrhage into gastrointestinal tract or intracerebral hemorrhage usually occurs when platelets < 10,000/mm³.

CLINICAL FINDINGS: ORAL
Mucosal
- Petechiae, ecchymosis (Figure 4-2)

Gingival/periodontal
- Gingival petechiae, spontaneous gingival bleeding.

Medical Management

Remove suspected causative drug, consider platelet transfusions when platelet count < 10,000/mm³, treat primary condition.

IMPLICATIONS FOR DENTAL/ORAL MEDICAL CARE: THROMBOCYTOPENIA
- Avoid aspirin and nonsteroidal anti-inflammatory drug (NSAID) therapy.
- Consult physician prior to surgical treatment.
- Platelet transfusions prior to dental treatment should be considered when platelet count < 50,000/mm³.
- Atraumatic oral hygiene when platelet count < 20,000/mm³. Consider chlorhexidine oral rinse for gingivitis control.

LIVER DISEASES

Hepatitis

Definition

Inflammatory disease of the liver.

Etiology

Viral hepatitis does not occur more frequently in the elderly population when compared with a younger population. When hepatitis B occurs in the elderly, patients are more likely to have an acute fulminant course. Non-A, non-B hepatitis (hepatitis C) may be acquired by an elderly individual during a hospital stay or via a blood transfusion.

Autoimmune hepatitis is generally a disease of younger adults (especially women), yet 20% of patients are aged 60+ years. Serological findings include elevated immunoglobulins (IgG) and circulating autoantibodies, including antinuclear antibody and smooth muscle antibody.

Drug-induced hepatitis has been attributed to multiple medications and becomes more severe with advancing age. In most cases, toxicity is stopped upon withdrawal of the drug. Alcohol-induced hepatitis occurs in the elderly but is considered uncommon. Liver damage by hepatotoxic medications is dose related and is characterized by a latent period following exposure. Typical medications are acetaminophen, alcohol, tetracycline, vitamin A, carbon tetrachloride, chloroform, heavy metals, phosphorous, and valproic acid.

CLINICAL FINDINGS: SYSTEMIC
Gastrointestinal
- Anorexia

Nausea
- Vomiting

Infectious/inflammatory process
- Abnormal liver function tests
- Abnormal serologic tests (viral hepatitis)
- Enlarged and tender liver
- Fever
- Flu-like symptoms
- Jaundice

CLINICAL FINDINGS: ORAL
Mucosal/gingival
- Lichen planus associated with hepatitis C
- Mucosal discoloration (yellow) caused by jaundice
- Petechiae and ecchymoses caused by liver dysfunction

Salivary glands
- Enlarged major salivary glands (Figure 3-34 in Chapter 3)

Medical Management

Viral hepatitis is managed by supportive care, rest, and treatment of associated complications. Interferon-alpha (IFN-α) has been used to treat hepatitis B and C.

Hepatitis C is often treated with Ribavarin plus interferon. Autoimmune hepatitis is treated with prednisone with or without azathioprine. Symptomatic improvement is often prompt with biochemical improvement of serum aminotransferases within 6 to 12 months and is predictive of histologic resolution (which can take 18–24 months). Drug-induced hepatitis is treated by discontinuation of the offending medication. Supportive measures and/or corticosteroids are indicated in certain patients.

IMPLICATIONS FOR DENTAL/ORAL MEDICAL CARE: HEPATITIS
- Viral hepatitis is associated with increased infections, bleeding, and diminished liver function.
- Medications metabolized by the liver should be used sparingly. The list of these drugs is extensive and includes amide anesthetics, acetaminophen, ampicillin, erythromycin, penicillin, and tetracycline.
- If a patient experiences corticosteroid-related adrenal suppression, supplemental steroids may be indicated (consultation with the physician is recommended).
- Patients on long-term corticosteroids are at risk of developing oral candidosis, and azathioprine can cause gingival inflammation in response to plaque.

Cirrhosis

Definition

Cirrhosis is the end result of liver damage that leads to fibrosis. Primary biliary cirrhosis (PBC) affects primarily females in the sixth decade of life. Antimitochondrial antibodies are present in 95% of patients. Hemochromatosis results from increased iron stores in the liver, usually occurs in males, and is rarely recognized before the fifth decade. The disease appears in women 10 to 20 years after menopause. Hepatocellular carcinoma will develop in 30% of older adults with cirrhosis.

Etiology

Alcohol, chronic hepatitis, PBC, and hemochromatosis

CLINICAL FINDINGS: SYSTEMIC
Alcoholic cirrhosis
- Enlarged liver/right upper quadrant abdominal pain
- Anorexia
- Nausea
- Vomiting
- Ascites
- Portal hypertension
- Signs of ethanol intoxication or withdrawal

Hemochromatosis
• Diabetes
• Arrhythmias
• Enlarged liver/right upper quadrant abdominal pain

Primary biliary cirrhosis
• Pruritis (most common sign)
• Often associated with Sjögren's syndrome

CLINICAL FINDINGS: ORAL
Oral mucosa
• Glossitis
• Angular cheilitis
• Mucosal discoloration
• Increased prevalence of oral cancer (alcoholic cirrhosis)

Salivary glands
• Sialadenosis (alcoholic cirrhosis)

Periodontal tissues
• Increased prevalence of periodontal diseases secondary to poor oral hygiene

Medical Management

Discontinuation of alcohol for alcoholic cirrhosis. Treatment of PBC is symptomatic, but certain medications used include cholestyramine (for pruritus), methotrexate, and colchicine. Hemochromatosis is treated by phlebotomy to deplete iron stores. Deferoxamine is used as a chelating agent and is excreted in the urine. Liver transplant is reserved for irreversible, progressive liver disease.

IMPLICATIONS FOR DENTAL/ORAL MEDICAL CARE: CIRRHOSIS
• Bleeding problems due to clotting factor deficiencies or thrombocytopenia.
• Inability to metabolize certain medications in advanced liver disease.
• There may be an induction of liver enzymes leading to a need for increased dosages of certain medications to obtain the desired effect.
• The patient with ascites may be unable to fully recline in the dental chair due to increased pressure on abdominal vessels.
• Liver transplant patients are on immunosuppressive therapy and are at risk of systemic infection of oral-pharyngeal origin, oral viral infections (herpes simplex, cytomegalovirus), and oral ulcers of unknown etiology.

NEUROLOGIC DISORDERS

Alzheimer's Disease

Definition

Idiopathic progressive and irreversible form of dementia characterized by memory loss and intellectual deterioration. It typically occurs after age 60, the prevalence increases with greater age, and there are an estimated 4 million people in the United States with Alzheimer's disease (AD).

Etiology

Unknown, although persons who have trisomy 21, a previous history of severe head trauma, or a first-degree relative with AD are at increased risk of acquiring AD. The diagnosis is made by excluding other possible causes of dementia, such as depression, drug toxicity, metabolic disorders, vitamin deficiency, and central nervous system infections. No laboratory tests are available; therefore, AD is diagnosed from clinical findings. *Probable AD* is diagnosed in adults aged 40 to 90 years when the problem begins, and patients have deficiencies in two or more areas of cognition that have progressively worsened, no disturbance in consciousness, and no other medical problem that could explain cognitive changes. A diagnosis of *definite AD* is made postmortem and is based on the presence of neuropathologic cerebral changes (neurofibrillary tangles and neuritic plaques).

CLINICAL FINDINGS: SYSTEMIC

Early stage
- Recent memory loss
- Inability to learn and retain new information
- Language problems
- Lack of spontaneity
- Errors in judgment
- Personality changes
- Difficulties in performing normal daily activities (eg, balancing checkbook, remembering direction to get to places)

Intermediate stage
- Progressive disturbances in speech, learning skills, decision making, and judgment
- Severe confusion in finding his/her way around the house
- At risk of frequent falls
- Agitation, hostility, uncooperativeness
- Loss of sense of time and place
- Perceptual problems (difficulties in recognizing his/her own face in the mirror)

Severe/terminal stage
- Apathy, disorientation, total dependence
- Incontinence
- Complete memory lost
- Aggressiveness/anxiousness and agitation
- At risk of pneumonia, malnutrition, aspiration, pressure necrosis of skin
- Coma and death

CLINICAL FINDINGS: ORAL
Increased prevalence of
- Poor oral hygiene
- Dental caries
- Periodontal diseases (Figure 3-3 in Chapter 3)
- Salivary gland hypofunction

Mental Status Examination

A simple neurologic examination (Table 4-5) begins every time the clinician evaluates the patient's appearance as he or she enters the office and carries on a conversation. The main components of a mental status examination (MSE) can be done in this initial greeting and include the appearance, speech, mood, perceptions, beliefs, fears, and cognitive state of the patient. The most important aspect is to compare the current neurologic findings with the baseline or "normal" for that patient.

Medical Management

Tacrine (Cognex) and donepezil hydrochloride (Aricept), rivastigmine (Exelon), and galantamine (Reminyl) are used symptomatically to slow down the progression of the disease in the mild to moderate stages. These drugs work by inhibiting the enzyme acetylcholinesterase and thereby increasing the amount of acetylcholine found in the brain.

IMPLICATIONS FOR DENTAL/ORAL MEDICAL CARE: ALZHEIMER'S DISEASE
Overall recommendations
- Medications patients are taking may cause salivary gland dysfunction, hypotensive episodes
- Caregivers must be trained to assist with daily oral hygiene
- Aggressive prevention programs, including topical fluorides, must be initiated
- More frequent recall appointments
- Short-acting anxiolytic benzodiazepines (eg, zaleplon, lorazepam, oxazepam) administered in reduced dosages before dental treatments may be helpful (Tables 4-6 and 4-7)

Early stage recommendations
- Treatment plans should be designed, anticipating oral decline
- Most routine dental care can be provided with only minor modifications
- Eliminate potential sources of pain, pathology, or sites of acute infection and restore to function as soon as possible

Moderate stage recommendations
- Expect uncooperative behavior
- Short appointments may be less stressful for the patient and clinician
- A thorough extraoral, intraoral, and radiologic examination may not be possible; the caregiver is necessary to provide symptomatic or objective information

TABLE 4-5.   BRIEF NEUROLOGIC EXAMINATION FOR ORAL HEALTH PROFESSIONALS

Area Assessed	Signs and Symptoms	Significance
Appearance	Self-neglect, inability to dress Level of activity (ie, high vs low) Gait disturbances Lethargy	May be due to confusion or apraxia (inability to perform purposeful movements) May reveal agitation or motor slowing Cerebellar ataxia (disorder or irregularity) Can occur in delirium or confusional state
Speech	Speaking rapidly Speaking slowly Speech unclear or slurred Trouble naming objects or jargon	Present in mania states Present in depression and dementia Dysarthria due to stroke or parkinsonian Aphasia due to stroke or Alzheimer's disease
Mood	Depression, hopelessness, worthlessness, feeling guilty Unduly cheerful, optimistic, or overconfident attitude Suicidal thoughts and intentions	Depression: suicide rates are high in elderly men, particularly if physically impaired May indicate a bipolar mood disorder such as manic depression Depression: psychiatric referral is indicated
Perceptions, beliefs, and fears	**Delusions** are false, idiosyncratic and ego-preoccupying ideas, eg, "Someone is stealing from me" **Obsessions** are recurrent unwanted ideas, compulsions, or unwanted behaviors that defy resistance **Hallucinations** are false visual, auditory, olfactory, or tactile perceptions (eg, hearing voices) **Phobias** are irrational fears of particular places, things, or situations (eg, fear of elevators)	Can occur in late life, schizophrenia, or paraphrenia Must be distinguished from culturally determined beliefs or hypochondriasis May indicate schizophrenia, neurotic or psychotic episodes in the elderly May also be the first sign of a severe depression Prominent in delirium, dementia, and schizophrenia and may occur in late-life depression and/or during grieving May be the first sign of severe depression

TABLE 4-5. BRIEF NEUROLOGIC EXAMINATION FOR ORAL HEALTH PROFESSIONALS		
Area Assessed	*Signs and Symptoms*	*Significance*
Cognition	Cognition is the capacity to think, reason, being aware, having perception and memory	Cognition is related to intelligence, depends on alertness, and is hampered by drowsiness, stupor, or coma.
Dementias,	Assessment involves testing attention, memory, and language functions	delirium, and depression are the most common disorders that affect cognition. Cognition is best tested using a quantitative assessment such as the Mini Mental Status

TABLE 4-6. ORAL SEDATION RECOMMENDATIONS FOR DEMENTIA PATIENTS	
Patient is already taking antiagitation medication	*Patient is not already taking anxiolytic/antiagitation drug*
Schedule dental treatment to coincide with the regularly scheduled drug (qd, bid, tid)	A short-acting benzodiazepine is recommended for mild-moderate dementia patients at reduced dosages. Start with low dose and increase slowly if needed.
If scheduled drug is prn, try using before dental treatment	
Consult physician about increasing dosage of scheduled drug prior to dental procedure	

bid = two times a day; prn = as needed; qd = once a day; tid = three times a day.

- Advise caregivers that daily oral hygiene will be their responsibility
- Treatment plans should be designed with minimal changes, not complete rehabilitation (eg, reline rather than remake dentures)

Late stage recommendations
- Avoid complex and time-consuming dental treatment
- Consider intravenous sedation or general anesthesia for necessary dental care
- Treatment must focus on removing unrestorable teeth and maintaining the dentition by frequent oral hygiene measures

		Onset	Half-Life
TABLE 4-7.	ORAL SEDATION RECOMMENDATIONS FOR DEMENTIA PATIENTS		
Drug	*Dose**	*(hours)*	*(hours)*
Benzodiazepines			
Oxazepam available strengths (10, 15, 30 mg)	10–15 mg	1.0–2.0	3–20
Alprazolam available strengths (1 mg/mL, 0.25, 0.5, 1, 2 mg)[†]	0.25–0.5 mg	1.0–2.0	12–15
Triazolam available strengths (0.125 mg, 0.25 mg)[‡]	0.25–0.5 mg	0.5–1.5	1.5–5.5
Lorazepam available strengths (2 mg/mL, 0.5, 1, 2 mg)[†‡]	1–2 mg	1.5–2.0	10–20
Sedative/hypnotics			
Zaleplon available strengths (5, 10 mg)	5–10 mg	0.5–1	1
Zolpidem available strengths (5, 10 mg)	5–10 mg	0.75–1.5	2–2.5

*Normal geriatric dose: ½ of normal adult dose if > 65 years old; ¼ of normal adult dose if > 75 years old.
[†]Available in liquid suspension.
[‡]Sublingual.

Non-Alzheimer's Dementias

Definition

Dementia is a permanent or progressive decline in several dimensions of intellectual function that interferes substantially with activities of daily living. Although new memory retention decreases with greater age, other cognitive functions remain relatively intact. Dementia represents a marked change from the age-dependent normal level of functioning.

Etiology

Usually follows injury severe enough to cause damage to the cerebrum's associated cortical areas. The etiology is categorized into three areas: structural, metabolic, and infectious (Table 4-8). The diagnosis of dementia is made by clinical

TABLE 4-8. ETIOLOGY OF NON-ALHEIMER'S DEMENTIAS

Structural	Metabolic	Infectious
Binswanger's dementia	Anoxias, chronic and	AIDS
Huntington's chorea	acute	Creutzfeldt-Jakob
Multi-infarct dementia	Hypercalcemia	disease
Normal pressure	Hypoglycemia	Gerstmann-Straussler's
hydrocephalus	Kidney failure	syndrome
Parkinson's disease	Liver failure	Syphilis
Pick's disease	Nutritional and	
	vitamin deficiencies	

AIDS = aquired immune deficiency syndrome.

findings with no available pathognomonic markers or laboratory tests. The diagnosis also implies that a marked change in the mental or intellectual capacities has occurred and that the condition is relatively stable.

CLINICAL FINDINGS: SYSTEMIC
- Has similarities to and differences from AD (Table 4-9). The course of the disease correlates with the etiology.

CLINICAL FINDINGS: ORAL
Increased prevalence of
- Poor oral hygiene
- Dental caries
- Periodontal diseases
- Salivary gland hypofunction

TABLE 4-9. NON-ALZHEIMER'S DEMENTIA: SIMILARITIES AND DIFFERENCES TO ALZHEIMER'S DEMENTIAS

Similarities	Differences
Impairment in speech (aphasia), motor activity (apraxia), interpretation of sensory input (agnosia), judgment, short-term memory, and attention span	Dramatic changes in personal habits or interests that occur without explanation
	In Alzheimer's disease, cognitive and behavioral changes occur gradually
Behavioral changes include agitation, anxiety, depression, apathy, irritability, and superficial euphoria	In dementia, changes can occur suddenly and are not necessarily progressive
	Gait abnormalities, seizures, incontinence, and muscle abnormalities can also occur

Medical Management

The critical factor is establishing an appropriate diagnosis, which will guide treatment. A psychiatric condition (eg, depression) may be a factor; neuropsychological, serologic, and radiologic tests may be required. Supportive care is required. Reevaluation of medications that have CNS activity is helpful.

IMPLICATIONS FOR DENTAL/ORAL MEDICAL CARE: NON-ALZHEIMER DEMENTIAS
- Use local anesthetics with epinephrine with caution when certain medications are being used (neurotransmitters, phenothiazines, antidepressants).
- Salivary hypofunction is caused by anticholinergics and antipsychotics.
- Dental professionals must educate caregivers and family members on oral hygiene and establish a frequent recall program.
- Follow guidelines established for AD (see above section on Alzheimer's disease).

Parkinson's Disease

Definition

Slow, progressive neurologic disorder characterized by tremors, rigidity, muscular weakness, and a peculiar gait. It appears most frequently between age 50 to 79 years, but the incidence declines above the eighth decade of life. The estimated prevalence is 1% of the population aged 50+ years, with an annual incidence of 50,000.

Etiology

Irreversible loss of dopaminergic neurons of the basal ganglia producing a deficiency of dopamine and a relative excess of acetylcholine. Dopamine inhibits the excitatory action of acetylcholine and controls the extrapyramidal (voluntary and involuntary) motor system. Therefore, the severity of symptoms is directly related to the degree of dopamine deficiency. Primary or idiopathic Parkinson's disease (PD) has an unknown etiology. Secondary or acquired PD is most likely caused by neuroleptic drugs (eg, phenothiazines, butyrophenones) or reserpine (antihypertensive, antipsychotic). These drugs cause PD through their dopamine receptor blocking properties. Other causes include toxic chemicals, infections, and other systemic disorders (eg, head trauma, cerebrovascular disease).

CLINICAL FINDINGS: SYSTEMIC
Neuromuscular
- Abnormal posture
- Bradykinesia (slow movement)
- Expressionless face
- Frequent falls
- Rigidity of striated muscles
- Tremor

Neurologic
- Disturbed mental cognition (late stage)
- Depression

Immunologic
- Increased susceptibility for pneumonia and urinary tract infection

CLINICAL FINDINGS: ORAL

Oral motor
- Drooling secondary to difficulties in swallowing
- Dysphagia
- Slow speech
- Tardive dyskinesia (involuntary oral-facial movements including lip smacking, grimacing, tongue flittering) caused by long-term therapy with levodopa
- Tremors of head, lips, and tongue

Oral mucosa
- Angular cheilitis

Salivary glands
- Xerostomia and salivary gland hypofunction secondary to anticholinergic medication usage (Figure 3-30 in Chapter 3)

Teeth and periodontal tissues
- Increased prevalence of dental caries and periodontal diseases (Figure 3-5 in Chapter 3)

Medical Management

Levodopa (L-dopa), the metabolic precursor of dopamine, is the most effective drug. Dopa decarboxylase inhibitors (eg, carbidopa or Sinemet) are used with levodopa to inhibit the rapid conversion of levodopa to dopamine. Anticholinergic drugs can help suppress mild tremors. In advanced PD, direct-acting dopamine agonists (eg, bromocriptine, pergolide, monoamine oxidase inhibitors) are prescribed. Other drugs used to treat tremors are antihistamines and beta-blockers, whereas tricyclic antidepressants assist in sleep and depression. In addition to drug therapy, supportive care with physical, occupational, and speech therapy is important to slow progressive disabilities.

IMPLICATIONS FOR DENTAL/ORAL MEDICAL CARE: PARKINSON'S DISEASE
- Antiparkinsonism drugs can cause salivary dysfunction.
- Excessive salivation may interfere with dental treatment.
- Frequent recall for prevention/early intervention of dental and periodontal diseases.
- Treatment planning should be based on a patient's mental *and* physical abilities.
- For medication-induced tardive dyskinesia, enameloplasty or a soft mouth guard may be needed to prevent irritations to the tongue.

- Greater physical assistance may be required due to uncontrollable muscle movements.
- Appointments should be kept short and relaxing to avoid aggravating muscle tremors and reduce involuntary jaw movements.
- Pretreatment anxiolytic agents and nitrous oxide analgesia may be helpful.
- Mouth props may be necessary for dental treatment.
- Intravenous or general anesthesia is an alternative for patients who have a severe loss of control over muscle movements.

ORTHOPEDIC DISEASES

Prosthetic Joint Diseases

Definition

Adults with painful and/or debilitating joint disease are often recipients of prosthetic joints. Approximately 450,000 total joint arthoplasties are performed annually in the United States. Deep infection of these total joint replacements usually results in failure of the initial operation and the need for extensive revision.

Etiology

Patients with total joint replacements are at increased risk of infection around these joints. In these infections, termed late prosthetic joint infections (LPJI), the etiopathogenic bacteria are typically *Staphylococcus epidermidis* or *Staphylococcus aureus*. These bacteria produce a complex carbohydrate mucoid slime layer that blocks the penetration of antibiotics, complement, and phagocytic cells. This protective slime may lead to the persistence and propagation of bacteria and hematogenous LPJI. However, the bacteria that are most often implicated in LPJI (*Staphylococcus*) make up a very minute percentage of the normal oral flora.

Bacteremias can cause hematogenous seeding of total joint implants, both in the early postoperative period and for many years following implantation. It appears that the most critical period is up to 2 years after joint placement. In addition, bacteremias may occur in the course of normal daily life and concurrently with dental and medical procedures. It is likely that many more oral bacteremias are spontaneously induced by daily events than are dental treatment induced.

Presently, no scientific evidence supports the position that antibiotic prophylaxis to prevent hematogenous infections is required prior to dental treatment in patients with total joint prostheses. The risk/benefit and cost-effectiveness ratios fail to justify the administration of routine antibiotic prophylaxis. The analogy of LPJI with infective endocarditis is invalid as the anatomy, blood supply, microorganisms, and mechanisms of infection are all different.

CLINICAL FINDINGS: SYSTEMIC

Bacteremias
- Bacteremias associated with acute infection in the oral cavity, skin, respiratory, gastrointestinal, and urogenital systems and/or other sites can cause late implant infection.

Unusual signs and symptoms
- In patients with prosthetic replacements, maintain a high index of suspicion for any unusual signs and symptoms (eg, fever, swelling, pain, joint that is warm to touch)

CLINICAL FINDINGS: ORAL
- None

Medical Management

The goal of management is to eliminate the infection in order to retain the limb and prosthetic joint and enable the patient to independently participate in activities of daily living. Therapeutic modalities include antibiotic therapy, incision and drainage of the infection, and, upon occasion, removal of the prosthetic joint.

IMPLICATIONS FOR DENTAL/ORAL MEDICAL CARE: PROSTHETIC JOINT DISEASES

Antibiotic prophylaxis not indicated
- Dental patients with pins, plates, and screws
- Most dental patients with total joint replacements

Antibiotic prophylaxis indicated (Table 4-10)
- There is limited evidence that some immunocompromised patients with total joint replacements may be at higher risk of experiencing hematogenous infections (Tables 4-11, 4-12)
- Higher-risk dental procedures performed within 2 years post–implant surgery (see Tables 4-11, 4-12)
- Patients with previous prosthetic joint infections (see Table 4-11)

Notes on antibiotic prophylaxis
- Antibiotic prophylaxis does not ensure prevention of LPJI; it only reduces its probability of occurrence
- The risk of side effects from antibiotic prophylaxis must be carefully evaluated

Treatment of orofacial infection
- Any patient with a total joint prosthesis with acute orofacial infection should be vigorously treated with elimination of the source of the infection (incision and drainage, endodontics, extraction)
- Eliminate any possible sources of chronic bacteremia or septicemia
- Use appropriate therapeutic antibiotics when indicated

TABLE 4-10. SUGGESTED ANTIBIOTIC PROPHYLAXIS REGIMENS

Patient Type	Suggested Drug	Regimen
Patient not allergic to penicillin	Cephalexin, cephradine, or amoxicillin	2 g orally 1 hour prior to procedure
Patients not allergic to penicillin and unable to take oral medications	Cefazolin or ampicillin	Cefazolin 1 g or ampicillin 2 g intramuscularly or intravenously 1 hour prior to procedure
Patients allergic to penicillin	Clindamycin	600 mg orally 1 hour prior to procedure
Patients allergic to penicillin and unable to take oral medications	Clindamycin	600 mg intravenously 1 hour prior to procedure

Other
- Identify the susceptible patient and determine invasive procedures most likely to create a chronic, significant bacteremia.
- Complete any necessary dental treatment prior to placement of the prosthesis.

TABLE 4-11. PATIENTS AT POTENTIAL INCREASED RISK OF EXPERIENCING HEMATOGENOUS TOTAL JOINT INFECTION

Patient Type	Condition Placing Patient at Risk
All patients during first 2 years following joint replacement	Any inflammatory or infectious process
Immunocompromised/ immunosuppressed patients	Inflammatory arthropathies such as rheumatoid arthritis, systemic lupus erythematosus Disease, drugs, or radiation-induced immunosuppression
Patients with comorbidities	Previous prosthetic joint infection Malnourishment Hemophilia HIV infection Insulin-dependent (type 1) diabetes Malignancy

HIV = human immunodeficiency virus.

TABLE 4-12. INCIDENCE STRATIFICATION OF BACTEREMIC DENTAL PROCEDURES	
Incidence	*Dental Procedure*
Higher incidence	Dental extractions
	Periodontal procedures, including surgery, subgingival placement of antibiotic fiber/strips, scaling and root planing, probing, recall maintenance
	Dental implant placement and reimplantation of avulsed teeth
	Endodontic instrumentation or surgery only beyond the apex
	Initial placement of orthodontic bands but not brackets
	Intraligamentary and intraosseous local anesthetic injections
	Prophylactic cleaning of teeth or implants where bleeding is anticipated
Lower incidence	Restorative dentistry with or without retraction cord
	Local anesthetic injections (nonintraligamentary and nonintraosseous)
	Intracanal endodontic treatment; post placement and build-up
	Placement of rubber dam
	Postoperative suture removal
	Placement of removable appliances
	Taking of oral impressions
	Fluoride treatments
	Taking of oral radiographs
	Orthodontic appliance adjustment

IMPLICATIONS FOR DENTAL/ORAL MEDICAL CARE: PROSTHETIC JOINT DISEASES

Occasionally, a patient with a total joint prosthesis may present to the dentist with a recommendation from his or her physician that is not consistent with these guidelines. This could be due to lack of familiarity with the guidelines or to special considerations about the patient's medical condition that are not known to the dentist. In this situation, the dentist is encouraged to consult with the physician to determine if there are any special considerations that might affect the dentist's decision on whether or not to premedicate and may wish to share a copy of these guidelines with the physician if appropriate. After this consultation, the dentist may decide to follow the physician's recommendation or, if in the dentist's professional judgment antibiotic prophylaxis is not indicated, may decide to proceed without antibiotic prophylaxis. The dentist is ultimately responsible for making treatment recommendations for his or her patients based on the dentist's professional judgment. The dentist can also request that the physician provide the antibiotic prophylaxis if (1) the physician insists on prophylaxis, and (2) in the dentist's professional judgment antibiotic prophylaxis is not indicated. Any perceived potential benefit of antibiotic prophylaxis must be weighed against the known risks of antibiotic toxicity, allergy, and development, selection, and transmission of microbial resistance.

Osteoporosis

Definition

Osteoporosis was most recently defined at the National Institutes of Health Consensus Conference as a skeletal disorder characterized by compromised bone strength predisposing a person to increased risk of fracture causing over 1 million fractures per year. It is a systemic skeletal disease that results in increased bone fragility. This disease affects more than 28 million people in the United States alone. Eighty percent of these are women. The disease is common in postmenopausal women but can occur for a variety of reasons in other age groups or in men.

Etiology

Changes in bone mass are brought about by an imbalance between bone resorption and bone formation, processes that are normally coupled. Once peak bone mass has been reached in the third decade of life, bone resorption generally outstrips bone formation, and there is loss of skeletal mass (Table 4-13). If bone mass becomes too low, osteoporosis results.

TABLE 4-13.   MAJOR PATHOGENETIC REASONS FOR LOW BONE MASS

Reason for Low Bone Mass	Predisposing Factors
Failure to achieve optimal peak bone mass	Largely genetically determined Can be affected by lifestyle (calcium intake and physical activity during skeletal growth)
Increased bone resorption	Estrogen deficiency is a major factor in women, especially after menopause Calcium and vitamin D deficiency and reduced calcium absorption in older individuals Endocrine abnormalities (eg, hyperparathyroidism or hyperthyroidism)
Inadequate bone formation	Due to complete loss of skeletal elements by excessive resorption, leaving no template on which to form new bone Age-related impairment of osteoblast function Changes in local and systemic factors that regulate bone formation

CLINICAL FINDINGS: SYSTEMIC
Onset
- Back pain in the thoracic or lumber spine subsequent to physical activity

Course of osteoporosis
- Highly variable
- Multiple fractures over time
- Progressive with loss of stature, persistent back pain, posterior curvature of the thoracic spine (kyphosis)

High-risk patients
- Postmenopausal women taking prolonged high-dose steroids; the risk of fractures is especially high

CLINICAL FINDINGS: ORAL
Bone
- Mandibular mineral content is reduced in subjects with osteoporotic features
- Decrease in mineral content of 30 to 50% is required before diminished bone density becomes apparent on dental radiographs
- Bone mineral density of buccal mandibular bone correlates with osteoporosis
- Reduction in cortical and subcortical alveolar bone density correlates with osteoporosis
- Osteoporosis increases the risk of mandibular fracture

Periodontal tissues
- Some studies suggest that systemic osteoporosis may contribute to periodontal attachment loss in the form of gingival recession

Medical Management

There are US Food and Drug Administration–approved drugs for the management of osteoporosis, which include calcium supplements, calcitonin, estrogen, and alendronates. Each of these drugs has a different mode of action to prevent bone loss, and each carries its own side effects that must be weighed against the benefits. The future of medical management of osteoporosis involves designing new drugs that will reduce bone loss, potentially restore bone mass, and show proven efficacy in preventing fractures.

IMPLICATIONS FOR DENTAL/ORAL MEDICAL CARE: OSTEOPOROSIS
- Decreased bone density width
- Enlarged bone spaces increase bone fragility, increasing the risk of mandibular fracture
- Denture-supporting mucosa in osteoporotic patients may become sensitive to trauma from the prosthesis; denture bases should be relined with a soft material and the occlusion carefully balanced
- Treatment with high dose biphosphonates increases the risk of developing osteonecrosis

PULMONARY DISEASES

Chronic Obstructive Pulmonary Disease

Definition

Chronic obstructive pulmonary disease (COPD) is a progressive decline in the function of the ventilation system, ability to exercise, and in the general health of the person with varying frequency by exacerbations of symptoms. COPD includes asthma, chronic bronchitis, and emphysema.

Etiology

COPD is very common in the elderly and the major cause is smoking. In the United States, COPD ranks among the 10 leading causes of death. Further, over the last 15 years, the incidence of COPD has risen more rapidly than that of any of the other nine leading causes of death. Approximately 3% of the United States population has chronic bronchitis, which is 1.2 to 2.3 times more prevalent in older persons than in younger persons; about 1% of the US population has emphysema. Asthma beginning in old age is uncommon.

CLINICAL FINDINGS: SYSTEMIC
Pulmonary
- Dyspnea on exertion
- Increased sputum production
- Chronic cough
- Wheezing

Metabolic
- Fatigue
- Weight loss
- Anorexia
- Fever

CLINICAL FINDINGS: ORAL
Oral mucosa
- Candidosis in patients taking inhalation corticosteroids
- Enlarged lymph nodes or scrofula present in patients with tuberculosis (TB)
- Periodontal tissues
- Attachment loss may be linked to COPD

Medical Management

Long-term treatment is directed toward controlling symptoms, maximizing independent self-care, and reducing the frequency of hospitalization. Medications progressively used in a stepwise fashion are anticholinergics, beta-adrenergics, bronchodilators, corticosteroids, and oxygen.

- Advisable to treat in semi-upright position
- Patient should bring inhaler medication to each appointment
- Maintain oxygen at level that is comfortable to the patient (if applicable)
- Avoid use of a rubber dam in severe disease
- Avoid nitrous oxide inhalation sedation
- If patients are taking corticosteroids, supplementation may be needed

Tuberculosis

Definition

Infection with *Mycobacterium tuberculosis* in 90% of cases involving the elderly is caused by reactivation of a primary infection or a newly acquired infection (eg, in a nursing home).

Etiology

Tuberculosis (TB) incidence is higher in elderly populations who represent the major reservoir for TB in the United States because these individuals were infected 50 to 70 years ago.

CLINICAL FINDINGS: SYSTEMIC
Pulmonary
- Positive purified protein derivative test; indicates previous infection
- Productive cough
- Bloody sputum

Metabolic
- Fatigue
- Weight loss
- Anorexia
- Fever

Other
- Many patients may exhibit no symptoms.

CLINICAL FINDINGS: ORAL
Oral mucosa
- Oral lesions are difficult to confirm
- Enlarged cervical or submandibular lymph nodes or scrofula present in some patients with TB

Medical Management

Antibiotics: combination of isoniazid, rifampin, pyrazinamide. The current recommendation for multidrug-resistant strains (resistance to isoniazid and rifampin) is to give two drugs that are active in vitro for at least 18 months. Resistance is suspected in (1) patients who have undergone previous courses of treatment (especially if compliance was poor), (2) patients with recently acquired disease, (3) immigrants from areas endemic for resistant strains, and (4) persons who acquire the infection from contact with above-mentioned sources.

IMPLICATIONS FOR DENTAL/ORAL MEDICAL CARE: TUBERCULOSIS
- TB is communicable in its active state
- A thorough past medical history is the first step in detection
- If the patient has a definite or questionable history of TB, consider consulting the physician
- If the patient has a history of TB, and the present status is free of clinical disease, treat as a normal patient
- If the patient has active TB, treatment should be limited to emergency care in an appropriate facility (usually a medical center)

Pneumonia

Definition
Infection of the pulmonary parenchyma caused by bacteria or other infection agents. Bacterial pneumonia results in areas of air-space becoming filled with exudates, inflammatory cells, and fibrin.

Etiology
Bacterial pneumonia usually originates from aspiration of oralpharyngeal bacteria that causes infection due to compromised host defenses. Therefore, oralpharyngeal microflora, including bacteria of periodontal origin, may play a role. Aspiration pneumonia is a significant concern among the elderly. In community-acquired aspiration pneumonia, the common pathogens are the anaerobic bacteria that normally reside in the gingival crevices (eg, peptostreptococci, fusobacteria, and black-pigmented anaerobes formerly referred to as *Bacteroides melaninogenicus*). In institutionally acquired aspiration pneumonia, the usual pathogens are gram-negative bacilli, sometimes in association with anaerobes. Most cases of pneumococcal and gram-negative bacillary pneumonia presumably follow microaspiration and an occult event resulting in a fairly small inoculum of more virulent bacteria from the posterior pharynx. Large-volume aspiration results in a relatively large inoculum of oropharyngeal bacteria into the lower airways and is associated with conditions that compromise consciousness or cause dysphagia.

CLINICAL FINDINGS: SYSTEMIC
Pulmonary
- Shallow respirations
- Hypoxia
- Tachycardia

Metabolic
- Fatigue and weakness
- General malaise
- Weight loss and poor appetite
- Anorexia
- Fever

CLINICAL FINDINGS: ORAL
Oral mucosa
- Possible fungal infections due to extended antibiotic use

Medical Management

The principal therapeutic modalities are antimicrobial agents. The selection of antimicrobial agent is challenging yet important; therefore, the causative organisms must be identified prior to recommendation of specific therapy. Commonly used agents include penicillin and antistaphylococcal penicillins, first- and third-generation cephalosporins, erythromycin, aminoglycosides, and vancomycin for methicillin-resistant strains. Other therapy modalities include respiratory and other forms of supportive care and drainage of empyemas and large pleural collections. Recommendations are similar to those for younger patients with pneumonia, although the elderly require closer therapeutic monitoring. Potentially nephrotoxic drugs, primarily aminoglycosides, require particular caution, including serum monitoring and frequent measurements of renal function, and should probably be avoided unless an alternative non-nephrotoxic drug cannot be used. Older persons have reduced cardiac reserve; therefore, intravenous fluids and electrolytes and other forms of osmotic loading must be given cautiously.

IMPLICATIONS FOR DENTAL/ORAL MEDICAL CARE: TUBERCULOSIS
- Optimal maintenance of oral health, including prostheses
- Oral candidosis possible due to systemic antibiotic therapy

RENAL DISEASES

Definition

Renal disease is progressive destruction of kidney tissue that can lead to complete failure of urine excretion and specific hormone secretion. Diseases include nephritic syndrome, end-stage renal disease, azotemia, uremic syndrome, and advanced uremic disease.

Renal failure is a condition in which the kidneys cannot fulfill their function of discharging metabolic waste and of maintaining the fluid and electrolyte balance.

Ftiology

Acute renal disease and kidney ischemia are due to trauma, toxic agents, certain medications, or septicemia (Table 4 14). Chronic renal failure is due to underly-

TABLE 4-14. CAUSES OF RENAL DISEASE
Carcinomas
Chronic glomerulonephritis
Congenital defects (eg, pyelonephritis)
Diabetes types I and II
Drug-induced nephropathies
Hypertension
Infections
Kidney stones
Lupus erythematosus
Nephrosclerosis
Polycystic disease
Renal artery occlusion
Renal artery stenosis

ing kidney abnormalities and occurs from a multitude of pathologic processes leading to an insufficiency of renal excretory and regulatory functions. End-stage renal failure occurs when kidney function is < 10% efficient.

CLINICAL FINDINGS: SYSTEMIC
- Atheroma
- Congestive cardiac failure
- Hypertension
- Pericarditis

Gastrointestinal
- Anorexia
- Duodenitis
- Esophagitis
- Gastritis
- Nausea
- Peptic ulcer
- Vomiting

Neurologic
- Headaches
- Lassitude
- Lethargy
- Sensory disturbances
- Tremor

Dermatologic
- Exaggerated bruising
- Hyperpigmentation

- Itching
- Pruritis

Hematologic/immunologic
- Anemia
- Increased bleeding time
- Infection susceptibility
- Lymphopenia

Metabolic
- Electrolyte disturbances
- Glucose intolerances
- Hyperparathyroidism
- Lipid abnormalities
- Nocturia
- Polyuria
- Thirst

End-State Renal Disease
- Glomerular filtration rate is diminished (normal 120 cc/minute; in renal disease < 10 cc/minute)
- Blood urea nitrogen is increased (normal < 20 mg/100 mL; in renal disease > 45 mg/100 mL)
- Creatinine is increased (normal < 1.5 mg/100 mL; in renal disease > 5 mg/100 mL)

CLINICAL FINDINGS: ORAL
Oral mucosa
- Candidosis
- Dysplastic lesions
- Macroglossia
- Pallor of mucosa secondary to anemia
- Petechiae/ecchymoses (on tongue)
- Stomatitis
- Ulcerations

Salivary glands
- Ammonia taste
- Parotitis

Periodontal tissues
- Gingival hyperplasia (when on cyclosporine or calcium channel blocker)

Medical Management

Diet modification, fluid electrolytes, and acid/base balance. Advanced renal disease is usually treated by dialysis and/or kidney transplant. Judicious use of drugs metabolized in the kidney (eg, streptomycin, gentamicin, neomycin, tetracyclines, and NSAIDs). Hemodialysis is associated with a 70% mortality rate over 5 years.

IMPLICATIONS FOR DENTAL/ORAL MEDICAL CARE: RENAL DISEASE

- Renal disease may be asymptomatic; consider renal failure if a patient has hypertension, breathlessness, swollen eyelids, gastrointestinal complaints, peripheral edema, chronic fatigue, and anemia.
- For patients on dialysis, consult with the patient's physician before treatment and consider prophylactic antibiotics to prevent infection of the shunt (if applicable).
- Dental treatment should be scheduled on the day after hemodialysis or midway between dialysis sessions when the effect of heparin is minimal and the patient is able to respond to treatment-related stress.
- Patients have a high risk of hepatitis.
- Renal transplant patients are often on corticosteroids and immunosuppressants that may require glucocorticoid replacement therapy and antibiotic prophylaxis.
- No BP recordings should be taken on the arm that contains an arteriovenous shunt.
- Determine bleeding status prior to extensive dental-alveolar surgery.

RHEUMATOLOGIC DISEASES

Definition

Arthritis is the most common chronic condition in geriatric patients. It is the result of an inflammatory or degenerative process involving joints.

Etiology

The most common cause of inflammatory arthritis in geriatric patients is autoimmune disease (eg, rheumatoid arthritis, lupus erythematosus, Sjögren's syndrome). The most common cause of noninflammatory arthritis in geriatric patients is osteoarthritis (degenerative joint disease).

CLINICAL FINDINGS: SYSTEMIC

Rheumatoid arthritis

- Approximately 70% of patients are female
- Hands and wrists most commonly affected (Figure 4-3)
- Moving stiffness
- Elevated erythrocyte sedimentation rate (ESR)
- Positive rheumatoid factor (RF) and antinuclear antibody (ANA)

Osteoarthritis

- Weight-bearing joints (hips, knees, spine) commonly affected
- Negative ESR
- Negative ANA
- Negative RF

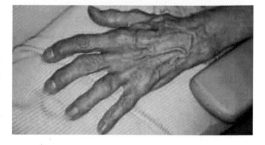

Figure 4-3
Compromised dexterity due to rheumatoid arthritis can affect proper oral hygiene.

Lupus erythematosus
- Systemic lupus erythematosus (SLE) more common in young women
- Approximately 90% of patients are female
- Chronic discoid lupus erythematosus (CDLE) commonly seen in older age in both genders
- Butterfly pattern rash in CDLE (rash on cheeks and bridge of nose)
- Malaise, arthritis, weight loss, rash, and pulmonary, cardiac, or central nervous system involvement may be present in SLE
- Anemia, leukopenia, thrombocytopenia may be present in SLE
- ANAs present in SLE (90%)

Sjögren's syndrome
- Approximately 90% of patients are female
- Xerostomia (dry mouth) complaint (Figures 3-27 and 3-51 in Chapter 3)
- Xerophthalmia (dry eyes; Figure 3-28 in Chapter 3)
- Connective tissue disorders (eg, lupus, scleroderma, rheumatoid arthritis) in secondary Sjögren's syndrome
- Kidney, thyroid, cardiac, central nervous system may be involved in the secondary Sjögren's syndrome
- Salivary gland enlargement (50%)
- Salivary gland hypofunction
- Dysphagia (difficulty swallowing)
- Dysphasia (difficulty speaking)
- Positive RF (50%)
- Positive ESR
- Positive ANA
- Positive anti SSA/Ro and SSB/La antibodies (25–70%)
- CD4 T cells lymphocytic infiltration of salivary gland tissue
- Diffused enlarged lymph nodes (10%) referred to as pseudolymphoma
- Non-Hodgkin's B-cell lymphoma may develop in 10% of patients with pseudolymphoma

CLINICAL FINDINGS: ORAL
Rheumatoid arthritis
- Temporomandibular joint disease (TMD) may be present.
- Limitation of mouth opening secondary to TMD.

- Dental caries and gingivitis can develop due to poor oral hygiene caused by dexterity limitation.

Osteoarthritis
- No specific findings.
- Dental caries and gingivitis can develop due to poor oral hygiene caused by dexterity limitation.

Lupus erythematosus
- Hyperkeratosis
- Ulcers
- Erythemic lesions (CDLE)
- Vesiculobullous lesions (SLE)

Sjögren's syndrome
- Angular cheilitis
- Caries—new and recurrent
- Dry lips and mucosa
- Eating difficulty
- Enlarged, tender major salivary glands (Figure 3-27 in Chapter 3)
- Intolerance to spicy and acidic food
- Lobulated tongue (Figure 3-51 in Chapter 3)
- Recurrent intraoral candidiosis
- Salivary hypofunction

Medical Management
Rheumatoid arthritis
- Rest, controlled exercise, splint
- Anti-inflammatory medications—NSAIDs, methotrexate, sulfasalazine, leflunomide, prednisone, and TNF-alpha blocking agents
- Surgery

Osteoarthritis
- Controlled exercise, reduced stress in affected joint, physical therapy
- Analgesics and anti-inflammatory medications
- Surgery

Lupus erythematosus
- Steroidal anti-inflammatory medications

Sjögren's syndrome
- Anti-inflammatory medications (see rheumatoid arthritis and lupus erythematous)
- Tear and saliva substitutes

Implications for Dental/Oral Medical Care: Rheumatologic Diseases

Rheumatoid arthritis

- Medications patients are taking may cause prolonged bleeding tendency, immune suppression, and increased susceptibility for oral bacterial, fungal, and viral infections.
- Patients with total joint replacement may need prophylactic antibiotics (see section above on total joint replacement)
- Patients taking methotrexate, D-penicillamine, and gold salts may develop abnormal liver function, complete blood count (CBC) values, or platelet count.
- Patients on steroids may develop adrenal suppression.
- More frequent recall appointments may be indicated based on the severity and sites of involvements.
- Modified oral health aids may be indicated (eg, modified toothbrush handle, dental floss holder; see Figure 4-1).

Osteoarthritis

- Not specific

Lupus erythematosus

- See section on rheumatoid arthritis under "Rheumatologic Diseases" (Figure 3-20 in Chapter 3)
- Appropriate diagnosis and management of vesiculobullous lesions (see Chapter 3, "Guide to Treatment of Common Oral Conditions," the section "Vesiculobullous Lesions of the Oral Mucosa")

Sjögren's syndrome

- Appropriate diagnosis and management of salivary hypofunction and xerostomia (see Chapter 3, section on salivary dysfunction and xerostomia).
- Follow up persistent salivary gland enlargement to rule out possibility of lymphoma.
- Labial minor salivary gland biopsy is the most reliable diagnostic aid.
- Multidisciplinary approach among ophthalmologist, rheumatologist, and oral health care provider is the most effective management
- Scintigraphy, serologic, and sialometric evaluations may be indicated as part of diagnostic work-up and follow-up to assess response to treatment.

ADDITIONAL READINGS

American Dental Association and American Academy of Orthopedic Surgeons. Antibiotic prophylaxis for dental patients with total joint replacements. J Am Dent Assoc 2003;134:895–9.

Chobanian AV, Bakris GL, Black HR, et al. The seventh report of the Joint National Committee on Prevention, Detection, Evaluation, and Treatment of High Blood Pressure. The JNC 7 report. JAMA 2003;289:2560–72.

Clarkson JE, Worthington HV, Eden OB. Interventions for preventing oral mucositis for patients with cancer receiving treatment (Cochrane review). In: The Cochrane Library, Issue 4, 2003. Chichester, UK: John Wiley & Sons, Ltd; 2003.

Little JW. The impact on dentistry of recent advances in the management of hypertension. Oral Surg Oral Med Oral Pathol Oral Radiol Endod 2000;90:591–9.

Little JW, Falace DA, Miller CS, Rhodus NL, editors. Dental management of the medically compromised patient 6th ed. Missouri: Mosby-Year Book Inc.; 2003.

Mulligan R, Sobel S. Preventive oral health care for compromised individuals. In: Harris NO, Garcia-Godoy F, editors. Primary preventive dentistry. 6th ed. Upper Saddle River (NJ): Pearson/Prentice Hall; 2004.

National Oral Health Information Clearinghouse (NOHIC). Oral health, cancer care and you: fitting the pieces together. NIH Publication No. 02-4372. Revised June 2002.

Prevention of bacterial endocarditis: recommendations by the American Heart Association. JAMA 1997;277:1794–801.

Silverman S Jr. Oral cancer. 5th ed. American Cancer Society. Hamilton (ON): BC Decker, Inc; 2003.

5

PRESCRIBING MEDICATIONS FOR THE GERIATRIC PATIENT

The use of prescription and nonprescription medications rises dramatically with age. In dental patients, the use of drugs increases fourfold from age 18–33 to age 80. In 1984, 34% of all retail drugs were consumed by persons age 65 or older, with an expected increase to 40% by the year 2030. Polypharmacy (multiple medications taken by a single patient) and inappropriate prescribing (wrong drug, dose, duration) are common in the geriatric population (Table 5-1). Ambulatory elderly patients take 3.1 to 7.9 medications simultaneously, rising in institutions to 3.3 to 8.6 medications per day (average of 7.2 drugs/patient), with 14% taking more than 10 drugs. One-third of elderly nursing home residents may receive 8 to 12 drugs per day, and 40% receive at least 1 inappropriate medication.

The intention of medical drugs is to stabilize or reverse disease processes. When they are taken properly and are working effectively, patients are actually safer for dental treatment than if they are not taking the drugs. There are several aspects of dentistry associated with adverse sequelae, particularly in older and medically complex patients. The most common aspect is stress. Stress leads to the flight or fight response, which elevates epinephrine levels, leading to increased blood pressure and cardiac rate and potentially overloading the cardiovascular system. Management of stress is accomplished by working in a competent and reassur-

TABLE 5-1. DRUGS IN THE ELDERLY	
Most Common Drugs Prescribed for Older Adults	Drugs Most Commonly Misprescribed in Older Adults
Analgesics	Amitriptyline
Antidiabetic agents	Analgesics
Cardiovascular agents	Benzodiazepines
H2-receptor antagonists	Dipyridamole
Immunosuppressives	H2-antagonists
Neuroleptics	Methyldopa

ing manner and in a calm environment. This is sometimes augmented pharmacologically with a sedative or antianxiety drug such as a benzodiazepine (see Chapter 4, "Dental Treatment Guidelines for Common Geriatric Conditions" the section on Alzheimer's disease, for further details).

It is also possible to create adverse drug reactions/interactions in geriatric and medically complex patients because of the drugs used in dentistry, but such occurrences are generally rare (Table 5-2). Medications used in dentistry are relatively safe for three reasons: (1) they are not particularly toxic, (2) they are used in a safe dose range, and (3) they are used for a relatively short time. The most common drug complications in dentistry are (1) increased bleeding in patients taking anticoagulants when aspirin or nonsteroidal anti-inflammatory agents (NSAIDs) are prescribed, (2) the risk of liver damage in patients with liver problems if acetaminophen or NSAIDs are prescribed, and (3) the risk of adverse pharmacologic interactions with drugs that are metabolized in the liver when erythromycin or ketoconazole is prescribed. In summary, it is relatively easy to avoid most drug-associated problems, particularly if the dentist has a reasonable level of awareness about the potential for physiologically and pharmacologically induced interactions.

Pharmacokinetic difficulties in the elderly arise primarily from changes in body composition and renal or liver function. With age, lean body mass declines and body fat increases, possibly affecting a drug's volume of distribution and, consequently, its elimination half-life. Drug metabolism is determined by hepatic function and blood flow. Liver blood flow decreases by 0.3 to 1.5% per year, with a potential 40 to 45% reduction at age 65 versus age 25. Renal function steadily decreases with increased age until reaching only 40% that of young adults. The glomerular filtration rate (GFR) may be significantly decreased, leading to an increase in the half-lives of drugs that rely on the renal route of elimination. Therefore, the selection, dose, and timing of drug administration in the elderly may require modification based upon age- and disease-associated changes in body composition and renal/liver function.

TABLE 5-2. DRUGS USED BY DENTISTRY MOST LIKELY TO CAUSE ADVERSE EFFECTS	
Drug	*Adverse effect*
Erythromycin, ketoconazole	Drug interactions
Aspirin and NSAIDs	Hemorrhage
Narcotics, barbiturates	Respiratory suppression
Metronidazole	Nausea if ingested with alcohol
Epinephrine	Increased cardiovascular stress

NSAIDs = nonsteroidal anti-inflammatory drugs.

Another potential problem in patients taking medications is adverse drug reactions, either locally in the oral cavity or systemically (Table 5-3). These problems can also directly cause oral disorders and/or impact dental management (Table 5-4). If a patient is taking a medication and there is concern about an adverse drug reaction, review the drug on the Internet or in a reference text (see suggested resources in Additional Readings).

Numerous nonprescription natural products and herbs are used by patients that have potential oral sequelae (Table 5-5). Clinicians need to document the use of these compounds and to be aware that some may have adverse effects on oral tissues and on the provision of dental care.

TABLE 5-3. POTENTIAL ORAL MANIFESTATIONS OF ADVERSE DRUG REACTIONS	
Abnormal pigmentation of gingival and mucosal tissues, and bone	Anticancer drugs
	Bismuth
	Estrogens
	Gold salts
	Minocycline
	Phenothiazines
	Tetracycline
Gingival hyperplasia	Calcium channel blockers
	Cyclosporin A
	Dilantin
Hemorrhage	Warfarin
	Heparin
Oral mucosal abnormalities	Angiotensin-converting enzyme inhibitors
	Antidiabetic agents
	Antiepileptics
	Barbiturates
	Gold salts
	Methyldopa
	NSAIDs
	Sulfonamides
	Thiazide diuretics
Salivary gland hypofunction	Antianxiety drugs
	Anticholinergics
	Antidepressants
	Antihistamines
	Antihypertensives
	Antiparkinson drugs
	Antipsychotics
	Chemotherapeutic drugs
	H2-antagonists

NSAIDs = nonsteroidal anti-inflammatory drugs.

TABLE 5-4. DENTAL MANAGEMENT CONCERNS OF DRUGS

Drug Groups	Example Medical Drug	Dental Management Problems
Anticoagulants	Aspirin, warfarin	Hemorrhage
Immunosuppressants	Corticosteroids Chemotherapeutic agents	Increased risk of fungal, bacterial, viral infections
Chemotherapeutic agents	Vincristine	Delayed healing Increased risk of infection
Antipsychotic drugs	Thorazine	Salivary hypofunction Involuntary mouth movements
Bisphosphonates (bone preserving drugs especially those used IV in cancer patients and even oral bisphosphonates used for osteoporosis)	Clodronate Alendronate	Slow bone healing or osteonecrosis

TABLE 5-5. NATURAL PRODUCTS THAT MAY ALTER DENTAL MANAGEMENT

Compound	Possible Oral Sequelae
Feverfew Garlic Ginger Ginko biloba Bilberry Dong quai St. John's wort	May increase hemorrhage
Echinacea St. John's wort	Inhibit liver enzymes potentiating the liver enzyme (cytochrome P-450) inhibiting effect of erythromycin and ketoconazole
Ephedra Ma-huang Kava-kava	May increase blood pressure and heart rate due to anxiety or if epinephrine/vasoconstrictor used
Valerian	May potentiate the effects of sedative-hypnotics and antianxiety drugs
Licorice	May potentiate the hypertensive- and edema-producing effect of corticosteroids

In summary, drug use in the elderly is complicated due to polypharmacy, altered pharmacokinetics, mental confusion, noncompliance, and communication difficulties. A thorough drug history is essential for safe drug use in the elderly, and clinicians should be cognizant of all drugs (prescription and nonprescription) an older person is taking before prescribing a new medication.

ADDITIONAL READINGS

Gage T, Pickett F, editors. Mosby's dental drug reference. St. Louis: Mosby; 2004.

Haas DA. Adverse drug interactions in dental practice: interactions associated with analgesics. J Am Dent Assoc 1999;130:397–407.

Hersh EV. Adverse drug interactions in dental practice: interactions involving antibiotics. J Am Dent Assoc 1999;130:236–51.

Moore PA. Adverse drug interactions in dental practice: interactions associated with local anesthetics, sedatives, and anxiolytics. J Am Dent Assoc 1999;130:541–54.

Moore PA, Gage TW, Hersh EV, et al. Adverse drug interactions in dental practice: professional and educational implications. J Am Dent Assoc 1999;130:47–57.

Wynn RL, Meiller TF, Crossley HL, editors. Drug information handbook for dentistry. Hudson (OH): Lexi Comp Inc; 2004.

Yagiela JA. Adverse drug interactions in dental practice: interactions associated with vasoconstrictors. J Am Dent Assoc 1999;130:701–9.

Internet Articles

Abdollahi M, Radfard M. A review of drug-induced oral reactions. J Contemp Dent Pract [serial online] 2003;1:10–31. Available at: http://www.thejcdp.com/issue013/abdollahi/01abdollahi.htm (accessed September 10, 2005).

Jacobsen PL, Chávez EM. Clinical management of the dental patient taking multiple drugs. J Contemp Dent Pract [serial online] 2005;(6)4:144–51. Available at: http://www.thejcdp.com/issue024/Jacobsen/01jacobsen.htm (accessed December 2, 2005).

6

NUTRITION AND ORAL HEALTH IN THE GERIATRIC PATIENT

Nutritional assessments of health in older adults have been underemphasized in primary care dentistry and medicine. However, due to the direct linkages between oral health and nutritional health, it is important for oral health care providers to be cognizant of the signs and symptoms of nutritional deficiencies and how improving oral conditions can have a positive influence on the nutritional health of an older adult. There are several specific nutritional deficiencies that have oral sequelae (Table 6-1).

TABLE 6-1. NUTRITION DEFICIENCIES WITH ORAL SEQUELAE	
Calcium deficiency	Skeletal osteoporosis of the mandible and (less likely) the maxilla
Niacin deficiency (pellagra)	The tongue becomes swollen and presses against the dentition
Vitamin B complex deficiencies	Changes in tongue, gingiva, lips, and mucous membranes
	With the exception of vitamin B_{12}, the B complex vitamins are not stored in the body; therefore, daily intake is important for oral and systemic health
Vitamin C deficiency (scurvy)	Edematous gingival tissues ultimately become hemorrhagic and ulcerated
	Teeth may become loose
	Gingivitis can be the source of halitosis
Vitamin D deficiency	Complicates calcium metabolism because vitamin D is required for calcium absorption
	Contributes to mandibular osteopenia or osteoporosis, particularly in edentulous mandible
Zinc deficiency	Possible taste changes
	Could result in a significant change in dietary intake of fluids and beverages

An older person's physical and mental condition and the medications used for systemic diseases have a profound impact on dietary selection and intake. Therefore, dental health professionals need to be aware of changes in medical problems, mental status, and medications in order to assist the patient in maintaining a well-balanced diet. For example, dementia and depression can have a deleterious influence on self-care, including the intake of foods and beverages and the performance of oral hygiene procedures. Polypharmacy is another common problem in the elderly, and drugs can cause multiple nutrient and oral health problems (Table 6-2) (see Chapter 5, "Prescribing Medications in the Geriatric Patient").

The use of removable prostheses may also have a profound influence on nutritional intake. Emphasis should be placed on encouraging the patient to eat a wide variety of foods (especially a diet high in fiber and calcium) rather than subsisting on pureed or liquefied foods. Soft diets tend to be rich in carbohydrates, fats, and sugars and are lacking in many nutrients, proteins, and fibers. If dentures are impairing dietary intake, adjustments may be required or consideration given to remaking the prosthesis.

TABLE 6-2. MEDICATIONS AND NUTRITIONAL PROBLEMS

Oral Health–Related Nutritional Problem	Drug or Drug Group
Anemia	Analgesics, phenytoin, antimicrobials
Appetite, decreased	Digoxin, captopril, NSAIDs, antihistamines
Appetite, increased	Insulin, lithium, prednisone
Dysphagia	Methotrexate, antineoplastics
Oral mucosal abnormalities	Angiotensin-converting enzyme inhibitors, antidiabetic agents, antiepileptics, barbiturates, gold salts, methyldopa, NSAIDs, sulfonamides, thiazide diuretics
Salivary hypofunction and xerostomia	Antianxiety drugs, anticholinergics, antidepressants, antihistamines, antihypertensives, antiparkinson drugs, antipsychotics, chemotherapeutic drugs, H2-antagonists
Taste changes	Antimicrobials, Tegretol, cholestyramine, antineoplastics, antiparkinsonisms, antipsychotics, captopril, Ca^{+2} channel blockers

NSAIDs = nonsteroidal anti-inflammatory drugs.

ADDITIONAL READINGS

Decker-Touger R, Sirois DA, Mobley CC. Nutrition and oral medicine. Totowa (NJ): Humana Press; 2005.

Saunders MJ. Nutrition and oral health in the elderly. Dent Clin N Am 1997;41:681–98.

Sheiham A, Steele J. Does the condition of the mouth and teeth affect the ability to eat certain foods, nutrient and dietary intake and nutritional status amongst older people? Public Health Nutr 2001;4:797–803.

Sheiham A, Steele JG, Marcenes W, et al. The relationship among dental status, nutrient intake, and nutritional status in older people. J Dent Res 2001;80:408–13.

Ship JA, Duffy V, Jones JA, Langmore S. Geriatric oral health and its impact on eating. J Am Geriatr Soc 1996;44:456–64.

I

APPENDIX

<www.medscape.com> This is a searchable site with an extensive medical-based home page that can be customized for your personal interests. It will send topics, such as pharmacology updates, to your computer and to allow you to keep current on areas of interest.

<http://www.fda.gov/cder/drug/drugReactions/default.htm> This site, within the FDA, provides information on adverse drug reactions.

<www.nlm.nih.gov> This site has a powerful search feature that looks at a large range of databases and searches out complete articles on specific topics.

<www.ada.org> The American Dental Association Web site contains resources and connects to a variety of medically related sites. Members can look through a long, well-researched list of useful Web sites related to drugs and health.

<www.healthgate.com> This site provides access to medicine searches as well as health news.

<http://www.dentalgate.com/dentistry/> This site has two different search features, one for the World Wide Web and another for medicine, especially designed for dentistry.

<www.personalhealthzone.com/pg000059.html> Prescription drug interactions and warnings relative to herbs and supplements.

<www.hiv-druginteractions.org> A site for HIV drug interactions as well as interactions with recreational/abuse drugs and with herbs.

<www.fda.gov/cder/drug/default.htm> The Center for Drug Evaluation and Research Web page has information on all drugs regulated by the FDA.

<www.drugs.com> This is a comprehensive and up-to-date prescription drug information site for consumers and professionals, with fast, easy searching of over 24,000 approved medications.

<www.rxlist.com> This site has a comprehensive list of drug indications, contraindications, interactions, etc. It also has an extensive list of medical diseases and how they are managed. Some of the explanations of the diseases are presented in a short video interview format, which makes it an interesting educational resource.

<www.fda.gov> This site provides multiple resources related to drugs. Several of the other sites noted above are within the <www.fda.gov> site.

<www.seniorcarepharmacist.com> This site focuses specifically on older adults and drugs.

<http://www.cochrane.org/index0.htm> This site provides evidence-based reviews on many clinical care issues, including Cochrane Reviews.

<http://www.xylitol.org> This site reviews the safety and efficacy of xylitol for the reduction of caries risk.

INDEX